open your heart

open your heart

12 Weeks of *Daily Devotions*

Martin Shannon

with Carol Showalter

PARACLETE PRESS
BREWSTER, MASSACHUSETTS

3D

Open Your Heart: 12 Weeks of Daily Devotions

2008 First Printing

Copyright © 2008 by Paraclete Press

ISBN: 978-1-55725-580-8

Unless otherwise noted, Scripture quotations are taken from the *Holy Bible, Revised Standard Version,* copyright © 1946, 1952, 1971 by the Division of Christian Education of the National Council of the Churches of Christ in the United States of America, and are used by permission. All rights reserved.

Scripture quotations marked KJV are taken from the King James Version of the Holy Bible.

Cover photo of Martin Shannon by Hans Spatzeck-Olsen.
Cover photo of Carol Showalter by Robert Tucker.

Library of Congress Cataloging-in-Publication Data

Shannon, Martin.
  Open your heart : 12 weeks of daily devotions / Martin Shannon, with
    Carol Showalter.
       p. cm.
    Includes bibliographical references.
    ISBN-13: 978-1-55725-580-8
  1. Devotional calendars. I. Showalter, Carol. II. Title.
    BV4811.S53 2008
    242'.2—dc22   2007050152

10 9 8 7 6 5 4 3 2 1

Published by Paraclete Press
Brewster, Massachusetts
www.paracletepress.com
Printed in the United States of America

Contents

Week One The Transparent Heart

Day 1   Hide and Seek

READ | Genesis 3:1–13

"[Adam] said, 'I heard the sound of thee in the garden, and I was afraid, because I was naked; and I hid myself.'" (v. 10)

"Amidst all of the instructions about obedience, the exhortations to persevere, and the admonitions against being unfaithful, it might be possible to forget that the way of discipleship is, first and foremost, about a *relationship*. All the methods and teachings and disciplines we can possibly follow are really of no value whatsoever unless, first, like branches attached to the vine, our lives are attached to Jesus Christ. That relationship is the only credible beginning and the only worthy end of the disciple's life."

These words, from the final day's reading of Session 1, make a fitting introduction to the twelve weeks of reflections for Session 2. We ended the daily readings of *Your Whole Life* with this essential reminder: the wholeness of our lives is dependent upon the wholeness of our relationship with God—with the One whose power made us, whose grace redeemed us, and whose love always intends the things that make for our wholeness and well-being. Our relationship with God is the North Star from which we take all the other bearings on our spiritual journey, and without which we are consigned to aimless searching and wandering.

What the Bible makes clear is that our relationship with God was dealt a severe wounding, a *breaking*, from almost the very beginning. In fact, all relationships suffered at the hands of Adam and Eve's rebellious choices. When the writer of Genesis tells us that, at first, the Man and the Woman were "both naked, and were not ashamed" (Genesis 2:25), he is describing so very much more than their physical condition. He is describing the condition of their hearts. Before God and before one another they stood entirely vulnerable and fearlessly transparent. But the joyful fellowship, even intimacy, that God intended for them—and us—to share with him and with one another was sacrificed for the sake of their own self-will and proud independence. Freedom of spirit and openness of heart were replaced with the burden of guilt and the hiddenness of fear.

You are probably reading these words because you already know something about freedom and openness, and you also know something about guilt and hiddenness. And you know which of these makes for a more joyful and whole life. It's just that getting from one to the other is not as easy as we would like. Thankfully, the Genesis story does not end with Adam and Eve's decision to hide from one another and from their Maker. God came to find them. "Where are you?" he kindly (and probably, persistently) calls out to those whom he loves (Genesis 3:8). The only sensible option is to answer. Perhaps reaching a hand out of the bushes, just far enough for it to be seen, is one way we begin to *open our hearts* and find our way back to God and to one another.

REFLECT | *Describe as best you can "where you are" in your relationship with God. How would you describe the level of openness you have with others, with those who are closest to you, and with those in your 3D group?*

Day 2   Open Your Hearts

R E A D | 2 Corinthians 6:1–13

Our mouth is open to you, Corinthians; our heart is wide. . . . In return—I speak as to children—widen your hearts also. (vv. 11, 13)

One thing that can certainly be said of the apostle Paul is that he was entirely honest and forthright in his relationship with his fellow Christians. His letters reveal a man whose passion for love and for truthfulness inspired every sentence he wrote, and this was never more apparent than when he had something difficult or even unwelcome to say.

There is a sense of estrangement between Paul and the Christians at Corinth as he writes this letter. We do not know all of the details, but of this much we are sure: the problem is severe and divisive, and, unless it is pulled up from the roots, it threatens to choke the very life out of this young church. So, Paul confronts the problem with characteristic directness—lovingly and truthfully.

What an example of wise diplomacy this entire letter is! There are allusions to the trouble, but always they are couched in a framework of positive, loving concern that Paul had toward these, his spiritual children. He knows that a necessary rebuke he has given has caused some of his readers to grow cold and resentful toward him. In their anger, some have questioned his motives and maligned his integrity. Even so, he writes with a sense of confidence that they are all still related to one another in Christ, and that the Holy Spirit of truth will eventually bring insight out of misunderstanding, and reconciliation out of discord. He opens his heart to his readers in the hope that they, in turn, will open their hearts to him and to one another: "our heart is wide—widen your hearts also."

The apostle Paul's approach is an example, and a great encouragement, to those who are looking for something deeper than superficially pleasant and polite relationships. Remember yesterday's reading. Adam and Eve were "designed" by God to live transparently with one another. This means, of course, that there are just as likely to be moments of conflict as moments of concord, just as likely to be moments of anger as moments of affection. But all of these "moments" can be steps toward a deeper, lasting, trusting, open relationship in Christ. Anyone who has once tasted the richness of this kind of fellowship rarely can be satisfied with anything less loving and honest.

In order to experience that kind of fellowship, we really have to open our hearts—"widen" our hearts, as Paul says—to one another. Think of your heart as the doorway into your life. Does it remain closed, or so small and narrow that no one can gain full access to the real you? Or, with a growing confidence in the power of God's love and truth, will you unfasten the bolts and open the way for others to find welcome?

REFLECT | *Does the idea of "opening your heart" appeal to you or frighten you? Why? Think for a moment about the various relationships that you have: which ones are superficial; which ones are deep and meaningful? What makes them so?*

Day 3　One Heart and Soul

READ | Acts 4:32–37
*Now the company of those who believed were of one heart and soul.
. . . (v. 32)*

The book of the Acts of the Apostles records the life of
the first-generation church, its missionary work, its values, its
sufferings, and its growth. But by no means does it present
some kind of utopian dream. Those early Christians knew a
fair share about conflict and dissent, as a complete reading
of this book reveals.

Still, there was no mistaking that something new and
different was taking place in the lives of these new believers,
and that the strongest evidence of their conversion was, in
fact, their relationships with one another. The newborn
church of Jerusalem exemplified the truth of Jesus' words,
spoken to his disciples on the night before he died: "By this
all men will know that you are my disciples, if you have love
for one another" (John 13:35).

The writer's description of this oneness of heart and
soul is intended to give us a taste, to whet our appetite for
the kind of Christianity experienced by those first believers.
Through the centuries, the church has referred to this as
a model of Christian community, one that has formed the
inspiration for Christian communities in every generation.
Don't you find it fascinating that among the very first signs
of the power of God's saving grace in Jesus Christ is the
depth of communion shared by his followers? If the Fall
resulted in our hiding from one another, then the Cross is
meant to bring us back together.

This is the promise, of course, but its fulfillment is not without difficulty. Today's Christian is just as apt to find him or herself living in isolation as did Adam and Eve. Individualism has so permeated the thinking of our time that none of us is exempt from its influence. For example, most of us are uncomfortable with, or even resistant to, any kind of authority over us, especially in spiritual matters. For all intents and purposes, we make ourselves the final court of appeal in all questions of dispute. Allowing others access into our lives, even by simply listening to the way that they see things (or see *us*), is still one of the most difficult tests we face.

The church has traditionally understood that when the writer of Acts says that no one claimed full ownership over his or her possessions, he was writing about more than just material goods. Giving to one another for the sake of the common good—for the sake of love—includes giving our thoughts and our wills, our opinions and our desires, as much as our time and our money. The fact that those first-century Christians were willing to open their hearts to one another in such a radical way is a testimony to the power of the gospel, and a challenge to the Christians of our own generation. You and I are descendents of this early community—we are its inheritors. So, how are we handling what has been passed on to us?

REFLECT | *Examine your own heart as honestly as you can. What do you find attractive about this image of Christian community? What do you find intimidating? Why?*

Day 4　A Simple Yes or No

READ | Matthew 5:33–38, 6:1
Jesus said, "Let what you say be simply 'Yes' or 'No'—anything more than this comes from evil." (v. 37)

In light of our reflections on what it means to have a transparent heart, here is a text worth pondering again and again. Some have interpreted Jesus' words as an instruction against the making of promises or vows of any kind. But this misses the point. It is not the *making* of promises that Jesus criticizes, but the *breaking* of them. Jesus is drawing a picture of a new kind of righteousness, one that "exceeds that of the scribes and Pharisees" (v. 20). This new righteousness is not the legalistic, hard kind of "rightness" that religious people sometimes display. It is an inner attitude that is without guile, without the desire to conceal or deceive. It is a righteousness that says what it means and means what it says. To the man or woman of integrity, nothing more is needed beyond a simple "yes" or "no." That, it seems, is the point being made here.

Our communication with each other should be so unreserved, so uncalculated, that all we need is a forthright and uncomplicated "yes or no" to express the truth of what we are saying. The problem, of course, is that our words are connected directly with our hearts—"for out of the abundance of the heart the mouth speaks," said Jesus (Matthew 12:34)—and, there, things are not nearly so simple. We cautiously measure our words because we are not so certain about what they will reveal or where they will lead us. We are afraid that we will be misunderstood; we do not entirely understand our own mixed feelings and motives; we do not want to commit to something without leaving ourselves a way out; we might say something that we really do not mean; or, we might say something that we really did mean, but did not mean to say. You see how complicated it all gets.

The answer is not to close our mouths and say nothing at all. The psalmist reveals a better way when he prays: "Search me, O God, and know my heart, try me and know my thoughts, and see if there be any wicked way in me, and lead me in the way everlasting" (Psalm 139:23–24). We do not always know if the "yes or no" of our lips reflects all that is in our hearts, for the heart that we know least is our own. Together with the psalmist, therefore, we depend upon the light of the Holy Spirit to acquaint us with the hidden depths of our mixed-up thoughts and motives.

Opening our hearts to God and to one another requires that we take a certain risk by opening our mouths. We do our best to simply express what we believe to be true, and then God uses—even blesses—our imperfect efforts and adds the light and guidance of the Holy Spirit to our human words and thoughts. He may confirm or correct the courses we are choosing, but in either case, the result is something of a miracle: increased self-understanding and deepened fellowship in Christ. Do not be afraid to seek this simplicity and openness of heart!

REFLECT | *Describe an experience when the words you spoke revealed (perhaps more than you wanted) the hidden thoughts of your heart. What is most difficult for you about making a straightforward commitment to do or not to do something?*

Day 5   The Healing Power of Confession

R E A D | James 5:13–20

Therefore, confess your sins to one another, and pray for one another, that you may be healed. (v. 16)

James is making a very powerful and a very hopeful connection here. Without claiming to understand exactly how, he is saying that sin and sickness have some kind of association. In some languages, the words for salvation and health actually come from the same root. Theologians have argued about this relationship for centuries, and we are not about to solve this mystery today. But of this much we can be certain—sin that is kept hidden in the dark eventually produces dis-ease and affliction, while sin that is confessed and forgiven eventually leads to peace and wholeness.

Think of a nasty cut caused by a sharp and dirty piece of metal. The temptation may be to quickly stem the bleeding, cover the wound, and get on with the business at hand— whatever leads to the quickest and most painless return to the normal living of the day. But by day's end, the sore is red and tender. Things are anything but normal. A closer examination reveals a dark metal filing, embedded inside the cut. No amount of first-aid cream or bandaging can bring relief. As long as that dirty particle of metal is there, the wound will fester and throb.

Confession for the soul is like the tweezers that reach into the body—sometimes by our own hand, but just as often by the hand of another, take hold of the offending fragment, and remove it from the messy wound. Now, free of infection, and with ever-lessening pain, the body finds that full healing can take place.

This analogy is not perfect, but you can see the similarities. Yes, a good deal of confession can take place directly between the soul and God. The tax collector who prayed in the temple, "God, be merciful to me a sinner" (Luke 18:13), had no need of witnesses in order to know heaven's grace. But, just as often, we need to seek out the presence of Christ in a brother or sister who will listen to our confession and audibly express to us the loving forgiveness of the Great Physician. In certain cases, when sin is particularly grave or sensitive (such as sins of a sexual or very personal nature), we need to seek out the wise and private counsel of a pastor or priest. More often, we can bring our self-inflicted wounds to the fellowship of our sisters and brothers, and there find all the forgiveness and help and healing that we need.

Healing comes in many ways, not the least of which is the relaxation and inner peace that grow out of a clear conscience. A great many of us unnecessarily endure distress and carry burdens that can be relieved through the simple admission to another person that we have done, said, or thought wrongly. Isn't it usually our pride—preserving our good image or fearing what others might think—that keeps us from humbling ourselves to confess before another human being the sin that is crippling us?

REFLECT | *Describe a time when admitting your wrongness to another person brought a sense of relief and joy. What had you "lost" by keeping the sin to yourself; what did you "gain" by confessing it? In what areas of your life do you know you are trying to protect yourself from humbly exposing your sin and need?*

Day 6 The Healing Balm of Forgiveness

READ | Psalm 32

Blessed is he whose transgression is forgiven. . . . (v. 1)

Yesterday we considered the image of an infected wound as one way of describing the effect of sin that goes untreated in the human soul. The first step toward wholeness is to open our hearts to the probing work of the Holy Spirit as God endeavors to pinpoint the source of the problem. If confession is like the sometimes unpleasant tool that reaches in and plucks our sin from the dark recesses of our souls, then forgiveness is the soothing balm that brings relief, comfort, and restoration to the wound it has left.

There are a number of psalms, including Psalm 32, that have traditionally been considered as "penitential" in nature (some others are Psalms 6, 38, 51, and 102). These are essentially prayers of confession, and the crux of their message is that opening our hearts to God includes honestly and humbly acknowledging our offenses. After all, God knows us even better than we know ourselves, and there is nothing about our lives that remains hidden from his sight. The idea that God *sees* everything about us is not meant to force us into fearful hiding (as Adam and Eve attempted to do). Quite to the contrary. God's all-knowing vision of our hearts is meant to bring us back to his side when we have strayed, back to our feet when we have fallen, back to wholeness when we are broken.

The psalmist describes the dismal condition of both his soul and his body when he vainly attempts to cover up his sin and hide his iniquity: I am wasting away; it is as if an

unbearably heavy weight clings to my shoulders; my strength
has evaporated like the sweat of my brow under the burning
sun; all I can do is sigh with discomfort. A dramatic picture,
to be sure, but anyone who has experienced even a portion
of what he is describing knows full well of what the psalmist
is speaking—*guilt.* To the untended soul, the poisonous
power of this insidious dis-ease is debilitating and eventually
lethal. There is only one antidote, and it comes from heaven
itself: "Blessed is he whose transgression is *forgiven!*"

It is as if the psalmist wakes up to his dreadful condition
and says, "Why am I living this way? As destructive and
inexcusable as my actions (my attitudes, my words, my
omissions) have been, there is nothing I have done that has
surprised my Maker. So, there is no point in my trying to act
as if nothing at all has happened. I will face up to my sin, I
will admit it to myself, and I will confess it openly."

No wonder the psalmist begins his song with the word
"blessed." He is giving testimony to the joy and freedom that
he himself has experienced. The medicine of forgiveness is
a guaranteed cure to the sin-sick soul, for its limitless source
is the very heart of God himself. The only cost to us is to
humble ourselves enough to ask for it.

REFLECT | *Administering the remedy of forgiveness goes both
ways—sometimes we must receive it, and sometimes we must give it.
Recall an example of both in your life and describe what took place.
To whom is it most difficult for you to say, "I am wrong; please
forgive me"? Why?*

Day 7   Bearing One Another's Burdens

R E A D | Galatians 6:1–10

Bear one another's burdens, and so fulfill the law of Christ. (v. 2)

Today we come back to one of the sweetest and most fulfilling fruits of living with a transparent heart—love. Certainly, learning to trust and to open our hearts to one another is not without risk. The story of Adam and Eve reminds us that hiding is "second nature" to us. But it also reminds us that we were made for intimate fellowship with God and one another, and that we will never be fully satisfied, we will never be whole, until we know once again the bond of love that unites us. Can there be any greater sense of fulfillment than what is found in the deep and genuine sharing of pain and joy, the mutual acceptance of one another with all our flaws and failings, the confidence that we can know and be known without any fear of judgment or rejection? Surely, this sense of communion is one of the great gifts God has given the Christian family.

Paul elevates this aspect of our life in Christ to the highest possible value when he writes, "Bear one another's burdens, and so fulfill the law of Christ." We hear an echo of the words of Jesus, teaching us to love God with all our heart, mind, soul, and strength. This is the first and great commandment, he said, and the second is just like it: Love your neighbor as yourself. To bear one another's burdens—to take into our own heart the weight of another's heart—is to become like our Lord himself. To treat another's needs as if they were our own; to be mindful of his or her interests and dreams, as if they were our own; to enjoy another's success as if it were our own—this is the kind of self-sacrificial investment that Jesus made in the lives of his disciples. At its most generous, it was an investment that led him to the most extravagant love of all: "Greater love has no man than this, that a man lay down his life for his friends" (John 15:13). Sometimes this is exactly what opening our heart to others feels like—like laying down our lives. It can be sacrificial and costly. But it can also be rich and rewarding.

Much has been said about the wonders of rapid communication and instant message sending. Computers and cell phones have put us at one another's immediate beck and call. But has all this technology made us any more personally committed to one another? Some have argued that modern technology has actually gotten in the way of genuine contact and personal investment, and that the world has grown increasingly impersonal even though advanced communication has made it ever smaller. In any case, one thing remains certain in every generation: the human heart longs for fellowship . . . genuine, deep, and abiding. Meeting with friends in a weekly group may seem artificial and contrived, but only if we fail to see beneath it the potential for opening our hearts to one another, for reaching out and connecting with someone else's life in a meaningful and life-changing way. There is certainly nothing artificial about that. In fact, ever since Adam and Eve lost that fellowship in the Garden of Eden, God has been about the business of planting new gardens wherever his people gather together. There he intends to grow fruit that will endure forever.

REFLECT | *What does it take for you to be invested in—to be sensitive and responsive to—the lives of others? What does it take for you to allow others to be invested in your life? In what specific way(s) is God asking you to lay down your life this week?*

Week Two Sometimes the Hardest
Person to Forgive is Myself

Day 1   Imperfect . . . and Still Loved

READ | Philippians 3:12–21

Not that I have already obtained this or am already perfect; but I press on to make it my own, because Christ Jesus has made me his own. (v. 12)

Last week, while reflecting on what it means to live with a transparent heart before God and one another, we began to look at the place of confession and forgiveness as building blocks for genuine fellowship in Christ. Communion cannot long endure under the stressful weight of unforgiven sin. Despite knowing this principle, our critical and sometimes hypersensitive natures can still be all too quick to rush to judgment and find fault with others. (Just consider the last time you lost something—whose name did you use when you called out, "_____, where's my _____?"). Just as often, however, we may harbor a deep, underlying, unforgiving attitude toward ourselves. In fact, a super-critical attitude toward others may actually be a symptom of our refusal to accept ourselves as imperfect.

Paul points to his own life to demonstrate both the problem as well as the cure. He was of a religious bent, we would say. As a boy, he was well trained in Jewish Law, and had taken it with great seriousness. He studied for the rabbinical ministry under some of the finest teachers of his day, and was numbered among the elite Pharisaic party. His zeal for righteousness finally led him to defend his Jewish faith with an aggression that knew no bounds. When he heard of the Christians, who seemed to be teaching some dangerous perversion of the Scriptures, he hastened to help those who were trying to stamp out the movement in its infancy (see Acts 9). But, with whom was Paul really fighting?

On the road from Jerusalem to Damascus, Paul met the living Christ, and his life turned from persecutor to disciple. There, under the blinding light of heaven, his eyes were opened to a truth that had, to that point, eluded him. "Since we are justified (made righteous) by faith," he wrote to the Romans, "we have *peace with God* through our Lord Jesus Christ" (5:1). What a wealth of meaning in that verse. It speaks of a settled rest, of a peace that passes understanding, of an utter confidence in and relinquishment to the mercy of God.

By the time Paul wrote to the Christians at Philippi, he had spent years in the service of his Savior. He was a hero in the eyes of those who had come to know the love of God through his ministry. In fact, the whole church knew his reputation as a faithful apostle of the Lord Jesus Christ. Yet, still, after all these accomplishments and at this late point in his life, he is content to say to his readers, "not that I have already attained it, or am already perfect . . ." (v. 12). He recognizes that he still has far to go, that he is still an unfinished sculpture in the hands of God.

What about you? Is being flawed really all right with you? How upset do you get when you fail at something, or when someone criticizes you? Are you striving so much for perfection that you miss the joy of grace? The apostle Paul was certain of one unchanging thing, despite his own imperfections: "Christ Jesus has made me his own." Can any number of defects detach us from the nail-pierced hands of Jesus?

REFLECT | *What about you? How do you feel about your faults, your weaknesses? Is the love of God really a free gift for you, or must you do something to earn it? What connection can you see between the way you see others, and the way you see yourself?*

Day 2   If Any One Does Sin

READ | 1 John 2:1–6

My little children, I am writing this to you so that you may not sin, but if any one does sin, we have an advocate with the Father, Jesus Christ the righteous. (v. 1)

There's that word again—sin. If it seems as if we are spending a lot of time discussing this uncomfortable subject, it is good to remember why we are doing so, because telling a Christian that he or she spends too much time dealing with sin is a little like telling a doctor not to spend so much time dealing with sickness. The fact is, sin is the chief obstacle to personal wholeness and loving fellowship with others. Ignoring it will not make it go away. Better that we face it, head on, identify its symptoms, examine its workings, and determine its causes. Then we can apply directly the only remedy that will cure the pain it causes—the forgiving love of God in Jesus Christ.

The truth is, many Christians find sin embarrassing. We can admit to the big generalization—"Yes, I am a sinner"—but we are less ready to admit to the specific act—"My friend, here is where I sinned against you." The great Bible teacher, F. B. Meyer, explains that this is because Christians have a "defective idea" about what sin really is: they would not hesitate to face up to their sin "if they realized what God's standard of holiness and sinlessness is; if they understood that sin consists in coming *short of his glory* as much as in distinct violation of his will; if they knew that there may be sin in motive as much as in act, and even in lack of love" (F. B. Meyer, *Great Verses Through the Bible*).

We may not even welcome such clarification, since it unmasks some of the thinly veiled excuses we make for ourselves: I was only trying to be helpful; I didn't actually mean to say that; I really wouldn't do anything to hurt you. If we are serious about our life as followers of Jesus Christ, then, sooner or later, just as he did with his own disciples, he will upset all our rationalizations and point out to us what is really stirring in our hearts. And when that happens, we must not mistake the disillusionment we have with ourselves for the displeasure of God. In fact, when my sin is disclosed, it usually turns out that the only person disappointed in me *is* me. Most of my friends already know my weaknesses quite well, and God is most assuredly familiar with every single one of them.

This is why John is so quick to remind his readers of *God's* answer to human sin. Yes, he writes, we should not sin. But, if we do, there is no need for us to defend ourselves, no need to make excuses or to paint a prettier picture than the one that suddenly appears before our eyes. God has provided a faithful advocate, Jesus Christ the only righteous One, and, in the face of our heart's disappointment, he will speak on our behalf. If he forgives us, than we have no choice but to forgive ourselves for being less than what we want to be, less than what we know we should be, and less than what we thought we were.

REFLECT | *What do you find most difficult about receiving forgiveness from God, and from another person? Think of an excuse you made for yourself in the past week. What was the purpose of making that excuse? If you put the excuse aside, with what are you left?*

Day 3   Who is to Condemn?

READ | Romans 8:31–39

Who shall bring any charge against God's elect? It is God who justifies; who is to condemn? (v. 33)

The eighth chapter of Paul's letter to the Romans is undoubtedly one of the most heartening and hopeful texts of the entire Bible. It begins, "There is now no condemnation for those who are in Christ Jesus." No condemnation—why is the apostle so passionate and persistent about assuring his readers of this truth? Clearly he has come to know human nature quite intimately. He knows himself, and he knows his fellow Christians, and, as a result, he knows our penchant for despair and self-reproach.

Isn't our fear of the judgment of others and, even more, the condemnation we level against ourselves, among the foremost causes of self-consciousness and anxiety? Paul seems to be saying, "Relax!"—remember who and what you are by recalling who God is and what he has done for you; do not forget from whence you have come, and for what purpose you were created; never doubt the power of God's love for you or its presence even in the most difficult of circumstances.

Every human life—every life—must endure its times of suffering. It matters not how prosperous and peaceful things may look in the lives of others. Thorns and thistles are now sown into the human condition. There is no escaping their sting (see Genesis 3:18). It is therefore imperative that you know, says Paul to his readers, that you have been claimed by God for his purposes; that he made you, has redeemed you, and is at work in you, even in the most discouraging moments; that he is able to work everything together for your good; and that absolutely nothing can separate you from his love.

The real "condemner" is none other than our old adversary, the devil, who, as Peter writes, goes about like a roaring lion, seeking those whom he may devour (1 Peter 5:8). He is in search of the weak and vulnerable places in our lives, and there he slings forth his fiery darts of accusation and temptation. Especially at those low times of great disappointment or fear, or when we have suffered hurt or embarrassment; and at those high times when we have enjoyed a surprising success or have bathed for a moment in the praise of others—these are the times when we are most at risk before the devil's attacks.

It is important to know that the real purpose of temptations at such hours as these goes beyond getting us to "act sinfully." Hell's deeper aim is to plunge us into condemnation and hopelessness, for that is the most effective condition for dampening our love of God and isolating us from the fellowship of our brothers and sisters. Is there any question now about why Paul's confident words carry such an urgent tone? Our spiritual lives depend upon their truth, and upon our adherence to that truth. You bemoan your imperfections, but who is there to condemn you? You have a Savior, and there is no power imaginable—including your own regrets—that can separate you from him.

REFLECT | *In what areas of your life are you most likely to experience condemnation? (Are they at all related to the areas where you are most likely to judge others?) Which of these verses in Romans 8:31–39 is most important to you? Why?*

Day 4   Having Mercy

READ | Matthew 5:1–11
Blessed are the merciful, for they shall obtain mercy. (v. 7)

There is a biblical phrase that appears numerous times in the Old Testament, describing God as "merciful and gracious, slow to anger, and abounding in steadfast love and faithfulness" (e.g., Exodus 34:6; Psalms 86:15, 103:8). To the Hebrews, mercy was first and foremost an attribute of God himself, a characteristic of the heavenly kingdom. This was especially true in two particular ways: in God's care and provision for his vulnerable creation, and in his forgiveness of sin. In other words, the mercy of God is seen in the compassionate aid he renders to those who are needy or helpless or undeserving. Of course, all of us fall within those categories and, from time to time, we are particularly aware of just how weak and unworthy we are. And though such times usually involve a good deal of grief and discomfort, they can also be the times when we are most aware of God's merciful love. Remember the words of the apostle Paul, who wrote: "While we were still weak, at the right time Christ died for the ungodly. . . . God shows his love for us in that while we were yet sinners Christ died for us" (Romans 5:6, 8). Jesus is the mercy of God in the flesh, and the Cross is the premier instrument by which he helps the helpless and favors the unfavorable.

Is it any wonder, then, that "the merciful" should be among the list of those most blessed in the kingdom of God? If mercy is an attribute of God himself, and Jesus is the expression of God's mercy, then we show ourselves to be citizens of heaven whenever we, too, are merciful—i.e., whenever we give aid to those in need or forgive those in our debt.

What is more, apparently mercy begets mercy—the merciful obtain mercy. It is tempting to think cynically that the thoughtful person gets taken advantage of and the "nice guy" really does finish last. But even in this world we know that the harsh and impatient person usually finds others to be harsh and impatient with him, while the person of compassion, the person who extends understanding and kindness, usually finds others wanting to return the favor. How much more will this be true in the world to come.

In the context of this week's theme—about extending forgiveness even to ourselves—this kind of compassion takes on even further meaning. There is a degree of patience we must learn to have with our own sins and shortcomings. This is not at all the same as excusing ourselves or simply not caring whether or not we do right or wrong in the eyes of God. It has to do with seeing ourselves as God sees us: dependent, weak, and always in need of the love of God. The merciful are those who know that they are walking through life empty-handed and who know, as well, that God has and will continue to provide all that they need. They know the weakness of their own condition and are therefore perfectly prepared to accept the weaknesses of others. Blessed are such people as these.

R E F L E C T | *Think of a time when someone was particularly understanding and patient with you. What did this feel like? What did it make you want to do or to be? Describe what makes you most impatient with yourself, and with others. Today, who is in need of your mercy?*

Day 5 I Have Calmed My Soul

R E A D | Psalm 130–131

But I have calmed and quieted my soul, like a child quieted at its mother's breast; like a child that is quieted is my soul. (131:2)

A quiet soul, as peaceful as a contented infant in the loving embrace of its mother—surely this psalmist must have been a parent who witnessed firsthand the hungry cries of a child changing into happy sighs at the breast of its mother. Is this not a fitting image for the kind of rest and delight for which our own souls long? Think for a moment about the many things for which your heart yearns. Isn't an abiding sense of inner peace among the very first things on the list?

Putting these two psalms together gives a complete picture of our own spiritual thirst turning into fullness in the arms of a loving God. But the "conversion" clearly begins with a cry: "Lord, hear my voice!" We do not know the psalmist's particular circumstances—what the "depths" were from which he wailed his prayer—but we can all identify with his tone of voice. There is a sense of acute desperation, even panic in his words.

Turning to God in our need is actually the first step toward healing. It certainly seems straightforward enough, and there are countless examples throughout the Bible. But even with all this evidence before us, including our own past experience, crying to God "out of the depths" actually takes some effort. Where is the first place you turn when you are "in trouble"? Like our spiritual parents in the Garden, we are likely to look first to our own devices to solve even the most insurmountable problems. This is because it is of the very nature of "depths" to be dark and foreboding, to be the places where we lose sight of all light and all hope. The depths make us feel that God is nowhere to be seen, and that he has probably stopped listening. The depths make us feel that we are all on our own.

What infant do you know, however, who is able to feed her own hungry stomach, or clothe her own naked body, or rock her own weary eyes to sleep? No father or mother deserving of the name would ever dream such a thing. The psalmist acknowledges that he stands utterly exposed and defenseless before a holy God. "If you, O God, were to concentrate only upon my sins and shortcomings, then there is nothing further to do. I may as well give up now." The psalmist's hope all turns on a single, tiny, and all-important word—"But . . . there is forgiveness with thee" (v. 4). The light for which he now patiently waits is the mercy of God, and its coming is as sure as the dawn.

There is no depth in a human life that is beyond the reach of God's steadfast love. There is no thirst that he cannot quench, no hunger that he cannot satisfy, and no distress that he cannot calm. We do ourselves severe harm if we ever think that there is anything we have done, thought, or said—anything that we *are*—that cannot be redeemed by heaven's grace. We are only children. Isn't it a bit foolish to expect more from ourselves than even our Heavenly Father does?'"

REFLECT | *In what area of your life do you especially long for contentment? For what "depth" are you tempted to think there is no solution? Why? What is it that God is asking you to believe about himself . . . about yourself?*

Day 6   God Forgets?

READ | Jeremiah 31:27–34
For I will forgive their iniquity, and I will remember their sin no more. (v. 34)

According to the prophet, there seems to be such a thing as divine forgetfulness. How are we to understand such a mystery?

Ironically, some Christians, particularly those who strive inordinately for rightness and perfection, fail to deal constructively with failure. It is of no benefit, of course, to sweep our errors "under the rug," so to speak, to pretend that they are not there or that they do not bother us. Eventually, our subconscious has a way of playing its nasty tricks, by reminding us at particularly vulnerable moments of our past failures. We may not immediately know the cause, but sometimes those self-conscious feelings, those over-reactions and anxieties, those fears and angers that suddenly arise in us are the harassing remnants of unresolved sin. For example, let's say that you lost your temper with a friend, but in your embarrassment you both go on with life as if nothing had happened at all. Sometime later, without any warning, a similar conflict arises, perhaps with someone else, and you find yourself nervous about saying anything at all. Now you are angry *and* fearful. Unconfessed and unforgiven sin has its way of bearing offspring.

As we have seen, the constructive way to deal with sin and failure is to humbly make your confession, receive forgiveness, and then ask God's help so that, as you are working to change your behavior, he is working to change your heart. Then we can move forward, freely and thankfully—cleansed, renewed, and strengthened. Having done with sin means letting go of the accusation, guilt, and despair with which some people flail themselves. (Of course, if some troublesome area of sin persists in our lives, we should seek a minister or priest who can listen to our confession and give us needed counsel and the assurance that God has indeed forgiven us. Pride can be a strong barrier to making such an open confession, but it should only be done with one who is trained and spiritually able to hear it rightly. It is very foolish to make intimate confessions to the wrong people.)

I will forgive their iniquity, and I will remember their sin no more. This is God's attitude toward our sin, once it is confessed and forgiven. It is *gone.* One Christian teacher used to say,

"God says that he will cast our sins into the depth of the sea."
With a smile she would add, "Then, I think he puts up a sign
that says, 'No Fishing!' " If God himself has "forgotten" our
wrongdoing, if God himself has "thrown it away," then who
are we to rehearse our failures, reiterate our weaknesses,
and fret about our imperfections? What we call remorse is
not the same as what the Bible calls repentance—the former
is the seed of discouragement and heaviness, while the latter
gives growth to freedom and change.

*What is the difference between "ignoring" and "forgetting" your sin?
What about the sins of others—is there any connection between what
you remember about others' offenses and what you remember about
your own?*

Day 7 　 Repentance, the Key

READ | Luke 18:9–14

*I tell you, this man went down to his house justified rather than the
other; for every one who exalts himself will be humbled, but he who
humbles himself will be exalted. (v. 14)*

In many respects, this story summarizes some of the
central elements in the teachings of Jesus. The story of the
Pharisee and the tax collector praying in the temple goes
to the heart of the gospel, the "good news," for it explains
the principal reason why God came to us in the flesh—Jesus
said: "Those who are well have no need of a physician, but
those who are sick; I came not to call the righteous, but
sinners" (Mark 2:17).

Before we judge the Pharisee too harshly for his pride and self-confidence, let us be sure that we understand what Jesus was saying about him. (Someone has said that there is no difference between the Pharisee's saying, "Thank you, God, that I am not like that tax collector," and our saying, "Thank you, God, that I am not like that Pharisee.") The truth is that the Pharisee did, in fact, live a more righteous life than the tax collector. His praying, fasting, and tithing were all according to biblical law and were faithful to Jewish tradition. He was not lying about his uprightness. In a sense, he had good reason to boast.

But it was not the Pharisee's moral rectitude that Jesus found defective. The heart of his problem is contained in the description of his prayer: "The Pharisee stood and prayed thus *with himself*" (v. 11). It was not that the Pharisee did not have some genuine things of which to be proud—it was that he did not need God. To his mind, his soul had no need of a physician, no need of a savior. Even in his prayer he was carrying on a conversation only with himself!

The tax collector, on the other hand, could barely bring himself to even approach God, much less speak to him. Jesus says that he stood at a distance with his head bowed and his eyes fixed upon the ground. He brought no list of accomplishments or good deeds, no record of successes or testimonies to his faithfulness. Apparently he did not even notice the Pharisee as he whispered: "God, be merciful to me, a sinner." There is no question as to the destitute condition of this man's soul. He presented no excuses, no desperate explanations, no promises of improvement. His only plea was for mercy.

Of the two men, said Jesus, it was this man who returned home justified. One meaning of the word "justify" is "to be pronounced free of guilt." The difference between the state in which these two men left the temple is this: one went away forgiven and free, while the other went away still bound in the shackles of his own self-sufficiency. So long as he remained blind to his own need, he would always be blind to the light of God's love.

We conclude this week's reflections on forgiveness—especially forgiving ourselves—with this graphic reminder of Jesus' perspective on sin. It is clearly not the same as our own. For while we are prone to wander back and forth between the two extremes of either excusing ourselves or condemning ourselves, God aims straight down the middle . . . and forgives.

REFLECT | *In what ways do you identify with the Pharisee? with the tax collector? This week, what, if anything, has changed about your understanding of sin and forgiveness?*

Week Three   The Hidden Bitter Root Of Jealousy

Day 1   Who Will Be First?

R E A D | Mark 9:33–37

They were silent, for on the way they had discussed with one another who was the greatest. (v. 34)

In the last two weeks, we have been discussing the indispensable place of confession and repentance for the sake of our own wholeness, as well as our relationships with others. The brokenness we have inherited since the Fall has left us all spiritually ill—too weak and willful in our relationship with God, and too untrusting and unloving in our relationships with others. Through his Son, God has done, and continues to do his part for restoring us to the fullness of health and fellowship and, as long as we have breath, it is for us to work with him toward those same ends. "Work out your own salvation with fear and trembling," wrote the apostle Paul, "for God is at work in you" (Philippians 2:12–13).

I know a man who suffered a heart attack some years ago. The cause was a blocked artery that prevented blood from delivering the vital oxygen necessary to feed the muscle of his heart. He is alive and well, but periodically he goes through a series of tests in order to determine if any new blockages are forming. He tells me that the procedures are mildly uncomfortable, but nothing whatsoever in comparison with the pain he felt on that day when he thought he might die. These regular examinations are what assure him that he may never have to face another day like that one.

In the coming weeks, we will be addressing more specifically some of those sins that can choke our spiritual hearts and cause such painful brokenness in the Body of

Christ. These are the pesky and destructive "foxes" that spoil the vineyards of the Lord (Song of Solomon 2:15)—things like anger, resentment, self-pity, fear, and, this week's nuisance, jealousy. We open our hearts to God and to one another so that we can honestly, even courageously, examine these sins for what they really are, and find their curative treatment in the loving forgiveness and power of God. So, let us begin.

There is a story about an old saint, an ascetic, who lived in the desert, and denied himself every form of carnal pleasure. The devil tried to tempt him with all sorts of pictures and allurements, but the man of God was too firmly fixed in his devotion to be swayed by them. Then the devil whispered in his ear, "Did you hear that your old friend, brother Ambrose, has been made bishop?" And across the saintly face, a scowl of envy and jealousy signaled that the devil had hit his mark!

As disciples of Jesus, we must face our personal jealousies. Even the first disciples expressed their fair share of this divisive sin, and apparently they did so in full view of their Master. How refreshing to know that they actually spoke openly with one another about the kinds of things that we only entertain in our thoughts. Jealousy seems to be one of those sins that are particularly difficult for us to confess, perhaps because, by doing so, we are admitting that we are lacking in some way. Nevertheless, the human soul is, by reason of its fall from original purity, tainted with jealousy. Some people have a greater struggle with it than others. But we all experience it from time to time. So the first thing to do is to recognize the "good news" of sin, which is that, like the twelve disciples, we *all* have the same question on our mind: who will be first?

REFLECT | *In what circumstances or with what people do you get jealous? What signs do you recognize that tell you that you are jealous? Think back to your childhood—who did you most want to surpass? Now who is it? Is there any connection?*

Day 2   The Sin of Lucifer

READ | Isaiah 14:12–20

You said in your heart, "I will ascend to heaven; above the stars of God I will set my throne on high . . . but you are brought down to Sheol." (vv. 13, 15)

Christian tradition has long taught that this passage in Isaiah refers to none other than the devil himself, Lucifer, the Day Star and son of the Dawn (v. 12). The prophet describes a glorious and shining angel who once stood at the right hand of God, but who, nevertheless, was not content with his creaturely status. "I will ascend above the stars of God," he ambitiously declared. "I will set my throne on high . . . I will make myself like the Most High." His fate, however, was to be cut down to the ground and cast into the depths of the Pit.

The tangled mystery of free will and sin's origins is too knotted for us to make any straight lines of it all. But this much the Bible makes clear—one of God's first angelic messengers fell from the heights of heaven because he wanted to become *like* God, *better* than God. Is it any surprise, therefore, that he would tempt God's first earthly children by suggesting the same desire? The serpent said to the woman: You will not die if you eat the fruit of this tree that

God has told you not to eat. He is only saying that because he knows that if you do eat it, "your eyes will be opened, and you will be like God" (Genesis 3:5). *Like* God . . . maybe even *better* than God!

And so it was that, by succumbing to the same deadly desire as did the devil—the jealous desire to rise above the limitations that God himself had set in place—our first parents sinned and fell from the light and from fellowship with God. Human nature has ever been subject to this subtle and powerful temptation to *be* God, to rule over others, to be preferred above all others, to be subject to no one, including God. It is the devil's own sin, tragically passed on to the children of men.

Certainly you and I are subject to the same temptation. Do you recognize it—perhaps when others are praised or advance beyond you; or, when you absolutely must make that new purchase like so-and-so has; or, when your best friend is put in charge of your committee? Some of our jealous reactions are petty and even humorous. "Keeping up with the Joneses" (better yet, passing them by) can get pretty ridiculous. But, we do well to remember that jealousy got its start as an act of bitter mutiny against the loving reign of God, and its flames have been stoked in the pit of hell ever since. Left unchecked (which means, unrecognized, unconfessed and unforgiven), it has caused, and can still cause, colossal damage to our own souls and to the Body of Christ.

REFLECT | *Where do you recognize jealousy's activity in your own life? One sign of jealousy can be dissatisfaction, restlessness, or ingratitude. How do you compensate for not getting what you want?*

Day 3   The Root of Bitterness

READ | Hebrews 12:7–17

See to it that no one fail to obtain the grace of God; that no "root of bitterness" spring up and cause trouble. (v. 15)

The letter to the Hebrews was written to a group of Christians who, because of suffering and difficulty, were tempted to renounce their faith in Christ and return to the old covenant. Again and again, the writer reminds them that God has fulfilled all of his promises in the person of his Son, and that what they stand to lose by going back is actually the answer to all of their longings. So, press on, he says. Countless others have gone before and are now watching as you make your own way to heaven. Do not turn back. After all, you have the example of Jesus Christ himself, who endured more pain and hostility than you can imagine. Now it is time for you to endure, and the trials you face are meant to strengthen, not to destroy, your faith. Stand and walk uprightly.

Then this cheerleader of the faith says something rather interesting and supremely practical: "Strive for peace with all men." The enemy of such peace he likens to a "root of bitterness" that suddenly springs up and causes all manner of trouble and conflict. All the time that they are facing trouble from without, they must be mindful that the only thing that can really destroy their faith and their fellowship is the corruptive root that arises from within . . . and jealousy is just such a bitter root.

The author's readers would be familiar with the story of Esau, who, he says, "sold his birthright for a single meal" (v. 16). If you recall, Esau craved the meal of his brother, Jacob, and greedily agreed to give over his birthright in exchange for it. (Jacob does not come out of this story looking so good, either.) Thus, says the writer of Genesis, "Esau despised his birthright" (see Genesis 25:29–34).

In your own cravings, warns the writer to these Hebrew Christians, do not succumb to the temptation to give away what is eternally important for the sake of an instant gratification that will soon pass away. The birthright of every Christian is the love of God in Jesus Christ, and that particular love that calls us by name belongs to no one else. Jesus loved us so much that he would have died for one of us alone! Such is the story we have in the parable of the lost sheep, where the Shepherd "left the ninety and nine in the wilderness" to go in search of the one sheep that was lost. Is not the bequest of heaven priceless? And will we jealously trade it in because we must have the "bowl of pottage" that is immediately before our eyes?

REFLECT | *Why is jealousy likened to "bitterness"? What do they have in common with one another? Is there some "root of bitterness" caused by jealousy that threatens to choke off your own spiritual life? What can you do about it? What are the "bowls of pottage" that tempt you most?*

Day 4   Sibling Rivalry

READ | Luke 15:11–32
There was a man who had two sons. . . . (v. 11)

The opening words of this parable tell you right away that there is going to be trouble! Two sons, one father. The question may never be put in exactly this form, but it is in every child's mind: will there be enough of Dad to go around?

Clearly the three parables contained in Luke 15 are making the point that God loves all his children so much, and so individually, that he will search high and low to find whichever one is lost, and will rejoice exceedingly, together with all of heaven, whenever the lost is found. Along those lines, Jesus easily could have ended the story of the prodigal son at the party thrown by his father. The point has been made—our Heavenly Father will leave us to our willful devices and foolish choices, but he will always be watching and waiting for our repentant return. And when we do come home, there will be no rejection, no reprisals, only loving welcome and merry celebration. We rightly treasure this picture of God as the waiting and forgiving Father who accepts us in all our unacceptability.

But Jesus does not end the story there. He has not yet told us about the second son, the eldest son, and, when he does, it is understandable if we are left to wonder who it is that is really "lost" in this family.

Years ago, a friend asked a retreat group to read this story and to write down the character with whom they most identified. He assumed that most everyone would name the prodigal, because they would recognize in his shame and in his repentance the testimonies of their own conversions back to God. To my friend's surprise, however, almost half the group said that they most identified with the elder brother, whose faithful work for his father went unrecognized and unrewarded. Plainly and simply, they thought, the elder son got a raw deal. It turned out that each of them had, in their relationships, some past experience when they felt that someone important to them had "gotten away with something" while, all the while, they had remained "good, true, loyal, and faithful."

Any of us with brothers and sisters, or sons and daughters, or very close friends, knows the tell-tail signs of sibling rivalry. Most all of us have experienced it, in our childhood and perhaps even as adults. We have competed for attention, approval, and favor, and when our "adversary" seems to have won out, with hardly any effort at all ("Dad/ Mom simply liked you best, and there was nothing I could do about it"), we may have tried other ways to win praise, or to make up to ourselves for what we felt was lacking.

The thing is, it seems quite apparent that the father in Jesus' story loved *both* his sons deeply and steadfastly. And neither one of them could do anything to deter that love. Unfortunately, however, jealousy knows no logic and submits itself to no amount of reason. When it thinks it has been slighted, it cannot be talked out of its reactions. The only effective solution is to confess it . . . and then to join the party.

REFLECT | *With which of the characters in the parable do you identify? What have been jealousy's effects in your own sibling relationships? How easy/difficult is it for you to rejoice in someone else's good fortune?*

Day 5   Is Life Fair?

R E A D | Matthew 20:1–16

These last worked only one hour, and you have made them equal to us who have borne the burden of the day and the scorching heat. (v. 12)

"It isn't fair!" How often have you said or thought those words? In some cases, you may have been absolutely right. There is such a thing, of course, as righteous anger against injustice and exploitation. The Bible, and especially the prophets' message, makes it perfectly clear that God sees everything and that his wrath is set against all injustice and unrighteousness. Truth to tell, most of us do not really burn with holy indignation at unfairness unless it affects us personally! What may seem like perfectly justifiable and righteous ire may actually be nothing more than jealousy in disguise. Of one thing we may be certain—how we are treated by others matters to us. Having said that, let us look at this parable of Jesus.

Many of the stories Jesus told were about the characteristics of the Kingdom of God, and this parable is among them. Like any good teacher, he used familiar images in order to explain unfamiliar ideas. The parables of the Kingdom were designed to introduce his listeners to a whole new "world" that did not necessarily operate according to all of the rules of this world. Through many of his stories, Jesus was turning their view of things upside down. That was certainly the case in this parable. Consider the main points:

In need of laborers, the householder goes out early in the morning and hires a group of men to work in his fields, and he promises to pay them a certain wage for the day. Later in the morning, he finds others without work and hires them also, promising simply to pay them "what is *right*" (this is an important phrase in the story). He repeats the same thing at noon, then again at three o'clock in the afternoon and finally again at five o'clock. By the end of the workday he has hired four groups of laborers, the last of which only worked for one hour. This is the group he pays first, and they receive exactly what he had promised the early-morning group. You can easily see why those who had worked for a full twelve hours would think, "Ah, he is going to give us more." But, the householder pays them only what they had agreed to—in fact, everyone receives the same wage, no matter how long they have worked—and that's when things get messy. "Unfair!" they cry, and it is safe to say that we would, too.

But, what is "fair," what is "right," from God's point of view? This is what the parable is really about—God's magnanimous favor and kindness. His limitless love is the measure of what is "fair" and "right," not our limited judgments. "Do you begrudge my generosity?" asked the householder. Can God not freely give his love in equal measure to all of his children, regardless of their worthiness or unworthiness? The truth is, that when jealousy penetrates our hearts, we do begrudge God's generosity to others. Jealousy actually blinds us to God's point of view. When we feel, for whatever reason, that we are "owed" something by God or by others, then jealousy is quick to accuse, "Unfair!" when payment is not forthcoming.

Even after saying all this, it is probably safe to say that we are still uncomfortable with this story. Why is that?

Day 6   If You Have Bitter Jealousy

READ | James 3:13–4:12

But if you have bitter jealousy and selfish ambition in your hearts, do not boast and be false to the truth. (3:14)

The letter of James is filled with practical directions for how to live in the world in faithfulness to God's word and the values of his kingdom. "Be doers of the word and not hearers only," it exhorts (1:22). So the author tackles some fairly dicey issues: how we speak to one another, what we ought to do with our wealth, our hypocritical words and actions, and the pride and ambition that cause divisions among us. Here is an interesting commentary on the passage we are considering today. It has to do with the problem of jealousy with regard to our ideas and opinions:

"True wisdom displays itself in a good life, particularly in 'gentleness' to the opinions and even the faults of one's neighbors. If anyone forgets this and is so absorbed in a sense of the sole correctness of his own opinions and a resulting sense of superiority as to feel bitter jealousy of his rivals and selfish ambition to be recognized as an exclusive leader, then when such a man claims wisdom, he is a liar." (Burton Scott Easton, *The Interpreter's Bible*, Vol. 12)

Remember, James is addressing some very down-to-earth issues, examining them from a very heavenly perspective. He sees rifts and rivalry in the Body of Christ and pinpoints "jealousy and selfish ambition" as one of the causes, especially with regard to claiming the superiority of one's own ideas. This, he says, is quite the opposite of that wisdom and openness that makes for peace.

Christian fellowship is certainly marred, if not destroyed, when we jealously maintain the correctness of our own points of view, and cling to the superiority of our own opinions. Even when our "facts" are objectively correct, it is possible that our *self*-righteous attitudes offend and hurt others. Consider some of the arguments that we have with one another. Usually, not long into the quarrel, the facts become of less importance than winning the battle. What we feel is at stake is more than the value of our opinion—it is the value of *me*. This is when "jealousy and selfish ambition" begin to lead the charge, and what began as a skirmish escalates into outright combat. By that point, we are actually fighting to raise ourselves above the other, perhaps in order to feel better about ourselves, but almost always at someone else's expense.

What is the solution? What you are doing through these twelve weeks is actually an essential part of it. Opening your heart to God and to one another—in humble honesty about your own needs, weaknesses, and sins—nourishes love for one another and actually helps us grow more comfortable with simply being wrong. The better we know that we are loved, by God and by others, the less we have to defend ourselves. Less is at stake. We can be gentle and merciful with others because they have been gentle and merciful with us. This is one way that we learn humility, which is one of the strongest weapons there is against jealousy.

REFLECT | *Think for a moment about how you feel about your own opinions and ideas. How do you feel when others agree with them? when they disagree with them? Locate the places where you are ambitious. What is it that is motivating you to "get ahead"?*

Day 7   It Was Out of Envy

R E A D | Matthew 27:11–23

For [Pilate] knew that it was out of envy that they had delivered him up. (v. 18)

Jealousy springs from a bitter root, and its fruits are also bitter. This week we have discussed jealousy's "origins"—its destructive power in the heart of one of God's angels, the inspiration it was in the fall of Adam and Eve—as well as some of its expressions—sibling rivalry, accusations of unfairness, quarreling, and ambition. We conclude the week's reflections by considering one of jealousy's most bitter fruits: the crucifixion of Jesus.

Sometimes conviction of sin, and the longing to be different that results from such conviction, is aroused within us when we become aware of the hurt it has caused someone we love. The sudden realization that a seemingly harmless, or at least justifiable, word or action on our part has actually inflicted pain upon another person gives us pause. It had not been our intention to wound, nevertheless we did. At such times, "what did I do?" is perhaps less of an important question than, "*why* did I do it?" It may very well be that the "why" was more injurious than the "what."

If jealousy had a personality, it would be that it likes to sneak around and go unnoticed and unrecognized, even disguising itself as something noble and righteous. The crowd that delivered Jesus over to be crucified seems to have been convinced that it was acting with the most religious of intentions. "This man has blasphemed against God, opposed the emperor, and disrespected the high priest; he deserves to be punished," they reasoned. But even Pontius Pilate knew better. The bloodlust of the chief priests and elders of the people had to stem from something far more malicious than simply upholding the law. Pilate knew that "envy" is what drove the crowd to cry out, "Crucify him!"

Human jealousy was—and *is*—one of the things that nailed Jesus to the cross. It can be both conniving as it schemes and vicious as it acts, and, left unchecked, it will satisfy itself with nothing less than the elimination of its competitors. The Book of Proverbs states, "Wrath is cruel, anger is overwhelming; but who can stand before jealousy?" (27:4). It is, writes the poet, "as cruel as the grave" (Song of Solomon 8:6). Thus, we see the most graphic example of its effects in the brutal murder of our Lord—"it was out of envy that they delivered him up."

What comes, naturally, is a sobering realization when circumstances cause us to face the jealousy that lives in our own hearts. This is why humbly opening our hearts to the scrutiny of close friends, our brothers and sisters in Christ, and to the convicting and cleansing work of the Holy Spirit, is so necessary in order to pull it out by its tangled roots. Jealousy, writes the apostle Paul, is one of the earmark "works of the flesh" (Galatians 5:20); love is the "fruit of the Spirit" (v. 22). Is there any question as to which one we want growing and blossoming in our own hearts?

REFLECT | *What are some of the "disguises" that jealousy takes in your own life? Think back upon this week—when were you jealous of someone? What did you do when you realized it?*

Week Four The Modern-Day Idol

Day 1 The Resurrected Christ– The Center of our Lives

READ | Colossians 3:1–17

Put to death, therefore what is earthly in you: fornication, impurity, passion, evil desire, and covetousness, which is idolatry. (v. 5)

The letter to the Colossians is one of the apostle Paul's most upbeat and encouraging messages. At times he seems electrified with delight at the thought of what God has done for us in Christ, and by the hope that we now enjoy through the resurrection to live an entirely new and fruitful life. He explains that, in a spiritual sense, we all died and were buried with Christ and that, when he rose victorious from the tomb we all rose with him! This is the best news imaginable, because it contains the absolute guarantee that we can live according to a different power and standard than what the world has to offer. Since you have been resurrected with Christ, he urges, then aim for the things of heaven. Put to death what is earthly in you and put on what is divine. Make the center of your life the Lord Jesus Christ.

If you know something about God's covenant with the children of Israel, and their deliverance from slavery in Egypt at his mighty hand, then Paul's teaching has a certain familiar ring to it. Upon Mount Sinai, God set forth his law, instructing his people about how they were to live now that they were free. The first of those commandments was: "I am the Lord your God who brought you out of the land of Egypt, out of the house of bondage. *You shall have no other gods before me*" (Exodus 20:2–3). The most basic requirement of their new life was to put God first, above all other "gods."

Both the Old and the New Testaments are clear, therefore—the worship of "idols" is not simply the practice of pagan religions; it is the chief temptation of all God's people. And Paul gives us a clue as to its meaning when he says that "covetousness" is idolatry.

Covetousness, the dictionary tells us, is the state of having an inordinate desire for that which belongs to another. Whenever we love with an excessive, unlawful desire to own for ourselves, we are coveting. It stands to reason, therefore, that we are putting the thing that we covet in the place of God; we are making it a rival "god" in our hearts. God alone is to be the center of our affections, and when he is not, we are committing idolatry.

Idolatry, therefore, is the worship of something or someone in the place of God. *Anything* we place before the love of God is an idol—it could be our possessions, our reputation or status, another person, our job, our family, even our own "spirituality." We pin our hopes and affections on these persons or things because of how they make us feel, and what they attain for us. Ultimately, idolatry is nothing more nor less than ordinary self-love.

Put it to death, Paul insists. For the sake of putting Christ first and having no other lords before the Lord your God, put idolatry to death. This is the focus of this week's readings, for in order to eradicate idolatry from our lives we must first identify what the idols are that we have enthroned in our hearts. Open your heart once again, and let us begin the search.

REFLECT | *Even before you ask the Holy Spirit's guidance, what are the things you suspect might be idols in your life? Describe what it feels like when you are covetous.*

Day 2   Wisdom Turned to Foolishness

R E A D | 1 Kings 11:1–13

And the Lord was angry with Solomon, because his heart had turned away from the Lord, the God of Israel, who had appeared to him twice, and had commanded him concerning this thing, that he should not go after other gods; but he did not keep what the Lord commanded. (vv. 9–10)

The reign of King Solomon was inaugurated with great hope and expectation. The first ten chapters of the First Book of Kings is an almost festive record of Solomon's good deeds and achievements. It had been the desire of his father, David, to build a temple for the Lord in Jerusalem, but it was Solomon who actually completed the deed. He loved the Lord, and when God asked him what the one thing was that he most desired, mindful of the burden he bore as the new king of Israel, Solomon prayed for an "understanding mind to govern thy people" (1 Kings 3:9). He was greatly respected for his wisdom, and widely known for his wealth and for the prosperity of his kingdom. But history records that Solomon's glory was not to last, and its darkening came at his own hand.

Solomon's ruin is traced to two fateful decisions on his part. First, the writer tells us, Solomon "loved many foreign women," taking into marriage many of the princesses of neighboring countries, in order to insure peace with those kingdoms. This was a case of human wisdom overriding the express command of God (see verse 2). Relying upon the logic of the day rather than upon the Lord of the universe, Solomon chose to disobey God's express will. This, in turn, led him to his second choice: under the influence of his foreign wives, he began to build altars, to burn incense, and to make sacrifices to their gods. Solomon *clung* to these wives in love (v. 2), and then he followed them as they led him away from the Lord his God.

> The poet Alexander Pope wrote:
> Vice is a monster of so frightful mien,
> As to be hated needs but to be seen.
> Yet seen too oft, familiar with her face,
> We first endure, then pity, then embrace.
> (*Essay on Man*, 1733–1734)

Removing God from the center of our lives is almost never done with a single, dramatic decision. The "vice" that leads us away from heaven usually presents itself in very reasonable form, and, over time, it becomes a comfortable companion. As was true of Solomon, our desire to be successful, to be at peace, to enlarge our circle of friendship, can lead us first to excuse the things we know to be wrong, and, ultimately, to practice them. When we excuse sin in others around us, because we do not want the conflict of standing for the truth we know and love, our own vision becomes blurred and our consciences numbed. Then, that which we first endure, we may eventually "pity, then embrace." Idolatry breeds idolatry, and soon the ways of God are all but forgotten. In Solomon's case, had he remained faithful and obedient to the Lord his God, he never would have begun that vicious cycle of decline in the first place.

REFLECT | *Identify some places in your life where you allow your human reason to discount the simple command of God. Where do you excuse others in order to avoid conflict?*

Day 3   A Mother's Idolatry and Its Fruit

READ | Genesis 27

Then Rebekah took the best garments of Esau her older son, which were with her in the house, and put them on Jacob her younger son. (v. 15)

The Bible is unblinking in the portraits it paints of its "heroes." No matter how much we look up to them, there is no glossing over of the weaknesses and failings of these men and women of faith. There is no question that we have as much to learn from their faults as from their faith.

The matriarch Rebekah had a favorite son. So, apparently, did her husband, Isaac, though that fact does not seem to figure so largely in the story. But Rebekah definitely preferred Jacob. Not content to let God raise Jacob above his brother, not even considering whether or not such elevation was God's will at all, Rebekah instigated a deceptive scheme in order to win (really, to steal) a blessing that rightfully belonged to Esau. (Although the men were twins, Esau was firstborn, a position that in those days gave him a distinct advantage when the father bestowed his paternal blessing.) The plan was successful. Isaac was deceived and gave his blessing to the second-born, Jacob. But that was not the end of the story. "Now Esau hated Jacob because of the blessing with which his father had blessed him," and planned to kill his brother in revenge. Again Rebekah intervened, fearing that she would lose both her sons if one should kill the other.

The point, of course, is that Rebekah's interference in the lives of her sons, and her obvious preference of one over the other, did much to cause friction, hatred, and alienation between these two brothers. Without doubt, they bore their own responsibility for the rivalry, but Rebekah's hand was definitely soiled with her sin of idolatry and control. As is true of so many well-meaning parents, her "help" often did more harm than good, because it was really motivated by selfish desires. It was not so much love for Jacob that compelled her to help him get ahead, as it was love for herself. Remember what idolatry actually is—putting something or someone before God, *for our own sake.*

God intervened and redeemed this situation, as he so often does. Esau came to know great blessing in his life, and Jacob (who was to become the father of the twelve tribes of Israel) was purged of his ambition through a long series of difficulties and sacrifices. Still, we can learn from their mother's mistakes. Manipulating others, especially our families, for our own selfish purposes, is never an acceptable means of parenting, though it is a very common one. It is one form of idolatry, for it reveals that we do not trust God with our children's lives as much as we may think we do. But God loves our children more than we do, and with a love that is entirely free of personal interest and ambition. He knows what is best, and our own scheming and control can only add confusion, pain, and delay in the working out of his purposes.

REFLECT | *Most of the manipulation we do with our families (or with others) is quite subtle. Where do you recognize it in your own life? What steps can you take to trust your family to God's will for them?*

Day 4   A Father's Idolatry and Its Fruit

R E A D | Genesis 37

Now Israel loved Joseph more than any other of his children, because he was the son of his old age; and he made him a long robe with sleeves. (v. 3)

Rebekah is not the only parent in the Bible whose preferential treatment of one of her children resulted in a good deal of pain and suffering. One might have expected that her son Jacob would have learned from his mother's example, but, then again, how many of us do? The presence of idolatry within our family relationships is neither an easy nor a comfortable thing to face. So the Bible gives us these vivid examples from among God's own favored people. From the records of their lives perhaps we can recognize some of the signs of trouble in our own.

It turns out that Jacob, the favored son of Rebekah, visited upon his own son some of the same preferential attitude he had received from his mother, not so much in the form of control (as was the case with Rebekah) as in outright favoritism. Not surprisingly, Jacob's preference for the young Joseph led to bitter jealousy and enmity with his older brothers, so much so, in fact, that they actually plotted to kill him. (Joseph, of course, did nothing to endear himself to his brothers when he "ratted" them out to their father, nor when he revealed his dream to them. Some things never change!)

The writer of Genesis clearly identifies the reason for Jacob's favoritism: Joseph was the son of "his old age" (v. 3)—something to be grateful for, but also something that had much more to do with Jacob than with Joseph. Can you see that in loving Joseph, Jacob was actually "loving himself," and that the superior attitude that Joseph had toward his brothers was the unfortunate result?

If they are honest with themselves, most parents will admit that one or two of their children "please" them more than the other(s). No matter how much effort is put into treating them all "equally," parental affection is not apportioned by a mathematical formula. This is because, like Jacob, we bring into our parenting the experiences and emotions that we ourselves had as children. It has ever been thus. Some of those experiences and emotions are still active, and they are still informing our attitudes and decisions. For example, some of you who read these lines may have felt yourself to be among the unfavored, and some have spent years striving fruitlessly to gain that preferred place. Others may have basked in the favored position.

In later years, God's dealings in the lives of Jacob and Joseph eventually changed both men. In Joseph's case, God allowed great and prolonged hardship to come in order to mature him and cleanse him from the effect of Jacob's idolatry. And Jacob suffered greatly at the erroneous report that Joseph had been killed in the desert. In both cases, it was the gradual maturing brought on by trial and testing that purified their love for one another, for the rest of the family, and for their God. There is no shame in admitting that our relationships, especially with the ones we love most, are tainted with self-interest and self-love. This is one of the areas of greatest need for all of us, and only the healing power of Jesus Christ can make of our relationships what they are meant to be.

REFLECT | *Look back on your childhood: what place did you have in your family? How does the way you were treated inform the way you treat others? If you are a parent, what decisions are you making about parenting that are drawn from your own experience as a child?*

Day 5   Who Is First?

READ | 1 Samuel 2:22–31 and 4:1–18

Thus the Lord has said, "Why then . . . honor your sons above me . . . ? (vv. 27, 29)

Raising children—training them in "the way they should go" (Proverbs 22:6)—is challenging all the time, can be frightening some of the time, and is always rewarding when a young soul begins to be formed in the ways of God. It can also be heartbreaking when that soul casts aside (if only for a time) the values and ideals that were planted within it in its youth. The story of Eli and of his sons is an example of the latter, and of a father's own unintentional role in the sadness. We have considered the ruinous effects of idolatry in the family when it takes the shape of favoritism and preferential treatment. It is important that we consider one further sign of idolatry's presence in family life.

Eli was a priest. Together with his sons, he was entrusted with the sacred duty of overseeing the prayers and sacrifices offered in the house of God. The writer of 1 Samuel tells us from the start that "the sons of Eli were worthless men who had no regard for the Lord" (2:12). How did they come to be in such a state, rejecting what their father surely had taught them? The message of the "man of God," who came to Eli in his old age, tells us succinctly that Eli, too, disregarded the Lord by honoring his own sons ahead of God. Here is how one writer describes the condition of Eli and his sons:

"There is always a difference between sentimentality in the handling of children and the sound preparation which is necessary for a life of service. So often the home is nothing but a cell of soft selfishness. Children do not learn within it the meaning of sacrifice and devotion and service. Parents, in their struggle to make their children better off, fail to make them better. Unconsciously they betray their own true ambitions. Anyone connected with education quickly recognizes how many children are spoiled by their parents' inverted pride. Materialistic standards of success control too many parental hopes, and consequently bring ruin upon distinguished family traditions. Eli was weak when he allowed Hophni and Phinehas to defame their office. He was content with the preferment their position gave them, instead of demanding from them any adequate discharge of their responsibilities" (John C. Schroeder, *The Interpreter's Bible*, Vol. 2).

In the case of Eli's idolatry, it was not that he preferred one of his children to the other; it was that he preferred both of his sons to God. Even while carrying out all of his religious duties, Eli was actually serving himself, and the bitter fruit of his idolatry was borne in the lives of his children. The conclusion of both their lives and their ministry was tragic.

It is essential that we honestly ask ourselves what we are really conveying to our children—by the way we live our own lives, by the things we really love and by the aims we really live for. Children, as you know, are highly perceptive.

Intuitively they can tell the difference, especially over the years, between what we say and what we really think. In the end, it is our own heart attitudes that form them much more than do our words. What is the message that our children are receiving from us? Is God first in our own lives? Or, by our own idolatry, are we subtly teaching them that it is all right to put ourselves first?

REFLECT | *This form of idolatry in family life can be very subtle and easily mistaken for genuine love, which is the sacred privilege and duty of every parent. What are you conveying to your children (if you are a parent) or to others around you, by the things you really love and live for?*

Day 6   Idolatry—Avoiding Truth

READ | 2 Timothy 3
But as for you, continue in what you have learned and have firmly believed. (v. 14)

Today's reading divides itself into two related sections—first, a bleak description of "the last days" (which the writer understood to include the time in which he lived), and second, an exhortation to live faithfully in the face of such difficult times.

The apostle Paul describes the last days as a time of great "stress" (v. 1). We all know something about stress in our personal lives, but Paul is saying that this type of stress will permeate all of society and that its essential cause will be unrestrained human sin. His list of offenses against God and neighbor is staggering, and seems to get worse as it goes on. The moribund condition of these "lovers of pleasure rather than lovers of God" reminds one of a disturbing story by Oscar Wilde, *The Portrait of Dorian Gray*. Wilde writes of a young man who gives himself increasingly to a life of utter self-pleasing, seeking to satisfy his own desires no matter the cost to those around him. Strangely, however, through the years he continues to appear young, strong, and healthy, as if his self-indulgence were preserving his vitality. All the time, however, a portrait of himself (which he kept carefully hidden away) grew increasingly grotesque, the painted face reflecting the spiraling decline of his soul toward complete disintegration and ruin. In the closing scene of the motion picture, Dorian destroys the portrait, only to find himself now appearing with all of its accumulated ugliness before he dies.

Paul himself is painting a portrait of the effects of sin in the world, of self-love gone rampant. This is idolatry that knows no limit. The condition of the human soul is not readily visible to us, but perhaps if we could see from God's point of view what sin does to us, we might be more willing to undergo the momentary pain of self-denial or the discipline of self-control in order to be changed and healed.

The second half of this chapter suggests that we can paint an entirely different picture of our lives, using the pigments of God's word. Paul is so bold as to present to his spiritual son, Timothy, a portrait of himself, of a life lived in faith, love, and steadfastness—and, yes, with persecutions and sufferings. There is no question but that the heart of the Christian life is the bearing of one's cross just as our Lord did. Paul essentially says that as we continue faithfully in "what we have learned," our experiences of self-denial and sacrifice will make room in our hearts for God's truth to do its re-forming work. This is the testimony of his very own life. If the last days will be filled with those who give themselves entirely over to their own wills and pleasures, and thereby "go on from bad to worse" (v. 13), they must also be filled with those who give themselves entirely over to God, and thereby become "changed into *his* likeness, from one degree of glory to another" (2 Corinthians 3:18). This is what Paul is urging Timothy to do. For, in the end, the only successful remedy for idolatry is an all-consuming love for God.

R E F L E C T | *What are the particular areas in your life where you know you have difficulty preferring God's ways to your own desires? What is the area where you are particularly concerned that you could become "ugly" if you do not change? What can you say about the value of self-denial in your own experience?*

Day 7   Idolatry and Insincerity

R E A D | Galatians 2

For before certain men came from James, [Peter] ate with the Gentiles; but when they came he drew back and separated himself, fearing the circumcision party. (v. 12)

Today's reading should encourage all of us who have a problem in the "good image" department, that is, wanting people always to approve of us. This chapter gives us a little insight into the spiritual struggles of two of the most distinguished Christians of all time—the apostles Peter and Paul. Despite all he had been through, Peter (or Cephas, as Paul calls him here) was still plagued by the desire to be approved of by others. Lest we judge him too harshly, we should remember that this seems to be a very common human characteristic. It becomes a real problem, however, when the approval of others means more to us than the approval of God himself.

Peter and the other apostles had gone on record with their conviction that God did not require Gentiles to be circumcised in order to be Christians, but there were some in the early church who did not fully agree with this, fearing that the traditions of the Jews would be lost. These were the so-called "Judaizers" who wanted all Christians to become Jews first.

Paul tells us that on a certain occasion, Peter (a Jewish Christian himself) was freely sharing a meal with the Gentile Christians of Antioch. When some Jewish Christians came from Jerusalem, Peter, fearing their disapproval, withdrew from eating at the table. Worse still, writes Paul, his actions led others to draw away as well, "so that even Barnabas was carried away by their insincerity" (v. 13). For the sake of looking good in the eyes of some, Peter turned his back on others.

The desire, even the genuine need, for the approval of others is common to us all. Paul confronted Peter, however, because obtaining such approval had become so important that he was willing to lay aside his own convictions and sacrifice some of his own friends in order to get it. This is another form of idolatry—of putting something or someone before God—because it says that what we think we *need* is of more value to us than what we *believe*. Furthermore, as in Peter's case, it sends a message to others, especially to those who may respect us or look to our example of faith. Regardless of what we say, are we telling others by our actions that there is nothing more paramount than the good opinion of others? Are we guilty of putting on an insincere face in order to be accepted? Are we sometimes guilty of saying behind someone's back what we would not say to his or her face? Or do we avoid doing or saying certain things in the presence of someone we know might not approve?

As we have seen this week, the modern idol takes many shapes, and all of them are formed of the same basic material—"me first." The wholeness God desires for us, and the unity he desires within the fellowships we share, can be fully realized only as we clear the shelves of our hearts of all the various idols we keep there. Someone once said that our god is whatever we love the most. Idolatry clearly identifies that god as "I." So, if we are to have no other gods before the Lord our God, then "I" must be taken down from the throne, and this is precisely what life in Jesus Christ is designed to do.

REFLECT | *Think of a time (even recently) when the desire for approval caused you to be insincere. In what other areas of your life do you put yourself before God? Why?*

Week Five Self-Righteousness

Day 1   What's Wrong with Being Right?

READ | Luke 15:1–7

I tell you there will be more joy in heaven over one sinner who repents than over ninety-nine righteous persons who need no repentance. (v. 7)

During our reflections on the subject of forgiving ourselves, we considered Jesus' parable of the Pharisee and the tax collector who went to the temple to pray (Week Two, Day 7). Did you notice to whom Jesus addressed this story? Luke tells us that he was speaking especially to those who "trusted in themselves that they were righteous" (Luke 18:9). *Self*-righteousness—the idea that our own efforts, noble intentions, and good deeds make us worthy of God's favor—is one of those sins that actually prevent us from knowing the depth of God's mercy as well as the gift of others' love. While few of us would easily admit it, and we may not display it as obviously as did the murmuring Pharisees and scribes, the notion that we are "sufficient" unto ourselves (or, at least that we *should* be sufficient unto ourselves) subtly permeates much of our thinking.

This week, we will spend some time considering self-righteousness, looking at the ways in which we depend upon ourselves for our own salvation. We will also consider the often misunderstood opposite of self-righteousness—humility. The psalmist wrote: "As a father pities his children, so the Lord pities those who fear him. For he knows our frame; he remembers that we are dust. As for man, his days are like grass; he flourishes like a flower of the field; for the wind passes over it, and it is gone, and its place knows it no more. But the steadfast love of the Lord is from everlasting to everlasting upon those who fear him, and *his righteousness* to children's children." (Psalm 103:14–17)

God "remembers" that we are dust, even if we forget from time to time. He is intimately aware of how feebly we stand and how perversely we wander, so his own expectations of our goodness and abilities are far lower than our own. Humility, which is the only genuine and lasting answer to self-righteousness, is about lowering our own expectations for ourselves, and raising them for God. As St. Augustine said, "O man, realize that you are man; all of your humility consists in knowing yourself."

Truly knowing ourselves, that is, accepting ourselves as deficient, is usually a problem in one of two ways: either we have such a high opinion of ourselves that we are blind to our faults and shortcomings, or we have such a low opinion of ourselves that our defects and failings are all we can see. In either case, *accepting* our fallen condition—embracing our own weakness and fallibility as ordinary sinners—is one way that we open our hearts to the grace of God. Repentance has little to do with scolding ourselves for tripping and falling. It has much more to do with allowing ourselves to be found and picked up by the love of God. Self-righteousness says, "I'm all right. I usually don't fall like this. Just give me a little more time and I can get up and find my way back." Or it says, "Just let me lie here. It's miserable, but I'm used to it. Maybe someday I'll catch up." But repentance calls out, "Here I am, over here," as we turn our faces away from ourselves and toward our Good Shepherd who comes to save us.

REFLECT | *With which side of self-righteousness do you most identify? What comes to mind when you think of the word "humility"? Is this a positive concept or a negative one? Why?*

Day 2   Whatever Was Gain to Me

R E A D | Philippians 3:1–14

I count everything as loss because of the surpassing worth of knowing Christ Jesus my Lord. (v. 8)

Paul's letter to the Philippians has been called the "Epistle of Joy," and a complete read of it will clearly reveal why. "Rejoice in the Lord always," he writes, "and again I will say, Rejoice" (4:4). Paul's words to this young church exude love for God, and a secure trust in his purposes, even when (*especially* when) circumstances are at their most difficult. Above all, Paul wants his own life, as well as the lives of his readers, to revolve entirely around Jesus Christ. He wants all other competitors for our affections, all other sources for our confidences, to take a far-distant second to our love for and hope in the Lord. What is more, he is absolutely certain that this is possible, not least of all because of his own experience of Christ's love for him.

Apparently, the Christians of Philippi have been hearing from some who suggest that there is more that they should be doing in order to be saved. Confidence in grace, they are being told, is not sufficient. Paul is indignant at the suggestion and presents the example of his own life as testimony to the fact that putting any "confidence in the flesh"—i.e., ourselves—is of no value whatsoever, and that the only glory we should know is the glory we have in Christ Jesus. Paul is making a blow at the most common self-righteous expression of all, pride.

If anyone has a reason to boast, writes Paul, it is he. His fine family lineage, his exceptional education, his moral accomplishments, and especially his religious fidelity and zeal, all combine to give him more than sufficient reason to be proud. Self-righteousness says, "These are the things that define me; these are the things that make me a person of value; and, some of these things actually make me more valuable than others." But the apostle knew that this could never be true; since he had come to know Christ Jesus his Lord, his value could never again be measured by his lineage or his accomplishments. When he met Jesus face to face on the road to Damascus, all these things seemed to fall away into nothingness. There, he was confronted by a Truth so lucid and undeniable that his own opinions and ideas fell to the ground. He was confronted by a Holiness so pure that all his own goodness shown tarnished and defiled. He was confronted by a Life so brilliant that he was blinded to everything but its Source. No wonder that he said to the Philippians, "From here on, what is before me—*Who* is before me—is worth everything. What is behind me is worth nothing."

The problem with self-righteousness is that it negates the grace of God; it diminishes the value of Jesus' death and resurrection. While self-righteous pride seeks to promote its own meager accomplishments and to rely upon them for a sense of security and self-confidence, humility looks elsewhere, away from its puny self, to find meaning and purpose. Humility says, "In the end, these things that I have made, and that have made me, do not matter at all. In fact, they are like so much soot. What predominantly matters is that Jesus Christ is in my life, and I am in his. He is worth everything to me, because I am worth everything to him."

REFLECT | *Identify the sources of your own pride. Be honest—what are the things that make you feel that you are valuable, acceptable, even superior to others? What is the difference between being "proud" and being "grateful"?*

Day 3   The Listening Heart

READ | Proverbs 12:15–19

The way of a fool is right in his own eyes, but a wise man listens to advice. (12:15)

The writer of the Book of Proverbs was apparently well acquainted with human nature. His ability to go straight to the heart of a matter, to identify the source of a problem and to give clear counsel as to the solution, show him to be someone who knew himself and others quite well. Much of what he writes has to do with wisdom, which may be understood as the capacity to live a life of integrity, love, and understanding; a life that begins, he says, with faith in God—"the fear of the Lord is the beginning of wisdom" (Proverbs 9:10). Obtaining such wisdom, however, is not a matter of study and learning; it is a matter of *listening*. The teaching of the Scriptures, said one of the Church Fathers, requires "an attentive ear."

Benedict of Nursia, the sixth-century monk whose work has defined much of Western monasticism for the past 1500 years, wrote a "rule" (a guidebook, really) that set forth the basic principles and instructions for a community's life and health. In it, he gives wise directions for everything from personal spirituality and discipline (prayer, Scripture reading, eating, and sleeping) to communal practices and traditions (greeting guests, observing Lent, manual labor). It is seventy-two chapters long, and it begins with this single word: *Listen*—"Listen, my son, to your master's precepts, and incline the ear of your heart" (*Rule of Benedict*, Prologue).

It sounds, does it not, as if Benedict had read the Book of Proverbs? "My son, if you receive my words and treasure up my commandments with you, making your ear attentive to wisdom and inclining your heart to understanding . . ." (2:1–2). "Listen to advice and accept instruction, that you may gain wisdom for the future" (19:20). "A wise son hears his father's instruction, but a scoffer does not listen to rebuke" (13:1).

The command to "listen" is about more than opening one's ears. It is about opening one's heart—making room within ourselves for the words of another because we know that our own words are not enough to help and to guide our lives. It is about being ready to receive a word of counsel or insight or correction from outside ourselves. This is never more difficult than when that word may be unexpected, unbidden, or even unwelcome. The "fool" rejects such advances out of hand. "I see things quite clearly on my own," he says. Foolishness and self-righteousness are siblings, as are wisdom and humility. The command to "listen" is really an exhortation to be humble, because it asks us to set aside the confidence we naturally place in our own view of things for the sake of hearing the voice of God, through whatever instrument it comes. The writer of Proverbs applied this principle to the making of a wise and faithful soul. Benedict applied this principle to the making of a strong and loving community. How does it apply to you?

REFLECT | *Through what voice(s) has God been speaking to you lately? What do you know to be the greatest obstacles to your own listening? What "words" have been most unwelcome to you this past week?*

Day 4   Praising the One True God

READ | Psalm 100

Know ye that the Lord he is God: it is he that hath made us, and not we ourselves; we are his people, and the sheep of his pasture. (v. 3, KJV)

The psalms have always played a substantial role in the worship and prayer of Christ's church. This is because they find their source in the hearts and experiences of God's covenanted people. The Book of Psalms was the prayer book of the Hebrew people, and, as such, its verses of song point us again and again to the Source and End of our lives. They tell us that the things that we see and feel and think are not the whole story, that behind and above and within our lives there is always the presence of our Maker and Redeemer. The intention of these prayers is to give glory to God both because of and regardless of the circumstances from which they are sung. They remind us that, in *all* times and places, "the Lord, he is God!" This is the jubilant shout of praise that cries out above all other noises.

This is why the psalms may actually be a helpful weapon in our fight against self-righteousness. For instance, consider the words of psalm 100. Look at the number of succinct commands to praise God that appear in so few verses: make a joyful noise, serve the Lord, come into his presence, enter his gates with thanksgiving, give thanks to him, bless his name! And all these imperative calls, all these activities, revolve around the one central and more interior entreaty to "know that the Lord, he is God." Just consider how much we could benefit from living according to that truth, every day. It is not that we do not believe that the statement is true; it is that we find it so difficult to be living all the time according to the wonder of it. And the psalmist gives us a hint as to why that might be.

There are two legitimate readings of the Hebrew in verse 3: "It is he that made us, *and we are his*," or, "It is he that hath made us, *and not we ourselves*." We have been talking about the very human (and very sinful) penchant for self-reliance, for making ourselves the answer to our own needs, and thereby "boasting" when things go well or "despairing" when they do not. Either reading of this verse (and both together) is a corrective to such self-righteous thinking. God is our Maker. Therefore, we belong to him and to him alone. Our lives are not of our own making. Can any one of us breathe into our nostrils the breath of life? Nor are our lives our own, to do with what we please. God has a loving plan for us, and whatever circumstances of success or failure we may experience, they all have as their ultimate aim the fulfillment of his intentions for our lives. Neither boasting nor despairing will make us humble. Both are signs that we have lost sight of who *we* are in the eyes of God, and therefore who *God* should be in our eyes. The humble are those who place all self-made plans—all successes and failures—under the reign of God's own purposes, because they know that, in every way, they have been made by God and belong to God.

REFLECT | *In the past week, when has your "boasting" or "despairing" blinded you to the presence of God in your life? Many of us are taught to take pride in being "self-made" women or men. How does this idea fit, if at all, in the Kingdom of God?*

Day 5   When Evidence is Ignored

READ | Jeremiah 2:20–37

Yet in spite of all these things you say, "I am innocent." (v. 35)

God recruited the prophet Jeremiah for an altogether unpleasant task. Because of its rebellion against the ways of God, the kingdom of Judah was on the threshold of its own destruction. Eventually, that threshold was brazenly crossed and, as a result, God's judgment descended upon the nation in the brutal form of its own enemies. But not before the prophet had a chance to repeatedly give warning about the severity of Judah's faithlessness and disobedience.

The prophet likened the nation to an unfaithful and adulterous wife. God himself was to be her husband, but she refused to give herself to him. Instead, she lustfully ran after other lovers (other gods), degrading herself in their service and staining herself with her shame before the eyes of heaven. It is a graphic and sordid picture of spiritual infidelity and apostasy. Still, despite the disturbing image, despite all the evidence set before her, Judah refused to acknowledge her guilt. Astonishingly, she said, "I am innocent" (v. 35). Jeremiah was chagrined: "How can you say, 'I am not defiled?' " (v. 23).

A good question. How is it that any of us can look squarely at the evidence of our own wrongdoing—the hurt we have inflicted on another, the failures of our own commitments, the lies we use to excuse our attitudes or actions—and still maintain that we are blameless? The prophet set forth a spiritual principle of the kingdom of God. God is willing and desirous to forgive sin, and even the most abhorrent of sins can be cleansed by his mercy. What defies his love, however, is the stubborn refusal to acknowledge our need of it. Even greater in God's eyes than all her sins of unfaithfulness was Judah's denial of her impoverished condition. "I will bring you to judgment," says God, "for saying, 'I have not sinned.'" (v. 35).

This is similar to the charge that Jesus laid before the scribes and the Pharisees. In their case, their outward actions might lead one to believe (and *did* lead them to believe) that they really were not sinners at heart. You are like freshly painted mausoleums, Jesus said to them, all good looking and attractive on the outside, "but within you are full of hypocrisy and iniquity" (Matthew 23:28). They were self-deceived. Their blindness to the presence of their own sin blinded them also to the presence of God's love. The one is a prerequisite for the other.

The apostle John wrote, "If we say we have no sin, we deceive ourselves and the truth is not in us" (1 John 1:8). Obstinate self-defense—the epitome of self-righteousness—is opposed to the forgiving grace of Christ. It is a prison house that keeps our hearts closed, locked up from the approach of God who, when he comes with convicting truth in one hand, always brings loving mercy in the other.

REFLECT | *Lately, where has God been working to convict you of your sin? How well are you receiving him? In what areas of your life are you the most defensive? In other words, what truth are you most resistant to hearing about yourself? Why?*

Day 6   True Righteousness

READ | Matthew 5:1–20

For I tell you, unless your righteousness exceeds that of the scribes and Pharisees you will never enter the kingdom of heaven. (v. 20)

By now we are getting the point. It is becoming clear that the Christian life is not meant to be a fierce and determined striving after perfection. Its clarion cry is certainly not, "I've got to be right at all costs." The cross that Jesus calls us to bear will most assuredly bring its crucifying hardships, but these are quite different from those that we inflict upon ourselves by anxiously clinging to the sufficiency of our own lives. The life of Christ's disciples is the "up and down" experience of real people who are happily aware that they have not yet arrived, but are glad to be on the way!

Scholars tell us that the main characteristic of the Pharisaic party was their rigorous adherence to the law. They inseparably linked the precision of their belief and behavior to their spiritual fitness in the eyes of God, and they were genuinely serious about observing correct religious ritual in every way. A second characteristic of the Pharisees was their respect for the traditions of the elders and their conformity to conventions passed down to them from the past. Thus, they were disturbed by an untrained teacher such as Jesus, who came saying things in a new way, and did not cite from the ancient teachers or rabbinic tradition. Instead, he claimed to be speaking on behalf of God himself and, based upon their conviction that no mere mortal could make such a claim, the Pharisees ridiculed and rejected him.

On the one hand, such an approach to faith seems initially reasonable, even commendable. But, says Jesus, it is not that this kind of righteousness is inherently wrong; it is that it is not *enough*. Jesus was actually requiring *more* than what the Pharisees were giving. The great early church teacher and pastor John Chrysostom said that "wherever the Holy Spirit is present, people of clay are turned into people of gold." The problem with the Pharisees was that they thought they were people of gold already, and that their own righteousness made them so. They thought that it was actually possible to adhere to God's laws in every way, and thus to enter the kingdom.

We should not be too quick to judge them. The temptation is common to us all to believe that our abilities and gifts and good will make us acceptable to God, if not superior to others. Reading the Beatitudes may be just the right corrective to such thinking, for they remind us just how *impossible* are God's standards. Meekness, purity of heart, mercy, righteousness—how is one to attain these divine characteristics on one's own? It is impossible to do so. And that is precisely the point. It *is* impossible to live the Christian life by one's own strength. Our hearts are not strong and agile enough to run such a course successfully. We need *more* than the righteousness of the Pharisees. The end of self-righteousness comes when we fall into the arms of our only Strength and Help. "In his days," wrote the prophet

Jeremiah, "Judah will be saved, and Israel will dwell securely. And this is the name by which he will be called: 'The Lord is our righteousness' " (Jeremiah 23:6).

REFLECT | *What Pharisaical attitudes do you recognize in yourself? Be specific. Which of the Beatitudes is the most appealing to you? which do you long for the most? which seems the most impossible for you? For which personal merits or achievements is God asking you to lay aside your claim for being acceptable?*

Day 7   He Came for the Un-righteous

READ | Matthew 9:1–13

For I came not to call the righteous, but sinners. (v. 13)

In a sense, we end the week where we began. On Day 1 we said that "*accepting* our fallen condition—embracing our own weakness and fallibility as ordinary sinners—is one way that we open our hearts to the grace of God." The fallen, weak, and fallible are precisely those for whom Jesus came. We are in good company!

Another way of putting it is this: Jesus came for those who are *wrong* and know it. His sacrifice is meaningless to those who believe that they are perfectly fine the way they are. Without an awareness of sin and need, there is no need of help and no desire for salvation. The sick seek out a physician; the wounded look for healing.

The joyful news of the gospel is that it is safe to face our sin—what we are, what we have done, what we have left undone—because we have a Savior. From him there is absolutely no condemnation. None whatsoever! Not our righteousness, but our *lack* of righteousness is what draws God's mercy and grace. Our wrongness appeals to his righteousness. Our inadequacy to make it on our own without him evokes his plenitude of grace, strength, and help in time of need.

Someone has said that unless we recognize our pain and bring it to speech, we are doomed to live without hope. People who are numb to their pain are also blind to their hope. What does that say to us who know our pain, our failure, or our need? It means that we experience hope, for we meet the One who touches us at the very point of our pain. He touches our wounds from our past, and heals them. He touches our guilt, and gives forgiveness. He touches our traumas, and sets us free from their oppression. And, perhaps more than we can know, he touches our hearts, and step by step converts us and brings us to greater wholeness. It would be foolish indeed to think that we had to provide all this healing, forgiveness, and freedom for ourselves. If you are in need of any of these—*because* you are in need of any of these—Jesus the Savior came for you.

REFLECT | *Where is it that you feel you simply cannot change? In what particular area of your life have you come to the end of hope in yourself? In what area do you have new hope?*

Week Six Who Me, Angry?

Day 1   *Be* Angry?

R E A D | Ephesians 4:22–32

Be angry but do not sin; do not let the sun go down on your anger,
and give no opportunity to the devil. (vv. 26–27)

    The overarching theme of these twelve weeks has to do
with the deepening and strengthening of our relationship
with God and with one another. If we are serious about
following Jesus, then this actually will be the "theme" of our
entire lives, for the life of discipleship is a lifelong journey
of learning and changing—learning the ways of God and
changing our own ways. As such, it is about so very much
more than changing our behavior. God intends for the work
of the Holy Spirit in our lives, and our cooperation with that
work, to re-make us in the image of his Son and our Savior,
Jesus Christ, not so that we can *act* like him, but so that
we can *be* like him. We open our hearts to God and to one
another so that this work can be done, so that by the light of
the Holy Spirit and the help of friends, we can locate those
dark and broken places that cripple our stride and weaken
our resolve. Our feet will walk more securely in step with
our Lord as our hearts come to beat more evenly in rhythm
with his own.

    The apostle Paul is referring to this transforming work
of the Spirit when he writes to the Christians of Ephesus,
urging them to put off the "old nature" of deceitfulness
and corruption, and to live according the "new nature"
of true righteousness and holiness (the likeness of God
himself). To help them in this endeavor, Paul identifies
some of the telltale signs of the old nature's crippling and

destructive work. Among them, he points to anger. One of the things that Paul says about anger, however, is somewhat unexpected—*Be* angry, but do not sin. *Be* angry? This seems odd. What is being suggested here? You may have noticed that the instructions the Bible gives at this point are all given within the context of one overriding directive: put away falsehood and speak the truth with your neighbor (v. 25). Being honest, being truth-full, is the reason for which being angry is entirely normal—because it is *real.* Our misguided attempts to repress or deny our angry reactions are one way in which we lie to ourselves and to others. A "good Christian," we say, does not get angry. Paul apparently takes exception to that statement.

Like all other human emotions, anger is a tightly woven thread in the tapestry of our humanity, and it cannot simply be detached without unraveling many other emotions with it. (Often, the people who suppress their angry feelings are also the ones who find it difficult to express other feelings as well, such as affection, grief, or zeal). If you are angry, Paul writes, then *be* angry. The most deadly and dangerous thing to do is to push it down and pretend that it is not there. For then, like a root fire, anger travels underground until it finds another outlet and bursts out on some unsuspecting target. Sometimes our overreactions, our unreasonable hurts and lost tempers, have at their source some unacknowledged, and therefore unresolved, anger from the distant or recent past. This is why Paul says, "do not sin; do not let the sun go down on your anger." Facing one's anger, admitting and sometimes even expressing it, is actually the constructive way toward resolving it.

REFLECT | *What do you think about anger? What experience(s) have you had recently when you were surprised at how angry you felt? What do you think was the source of your strong feelings?*

Day 2   An Angry Savior?

READ | John 2:13–23
And making a whip of cords, he drove them all, with the sheep and oxen, out of the temple; and he poured out the coins of the moneychangers and overturned their tables. (v. 15)

Before we go any further, perhaps we do well to be reminded that anger is something with which God himself is thoroughly familiar. Yes, we might say, God is obviously the only one who can "be angry" and never sin, but from that we should not conclude that somehow God is "too good" to be angry, as if the anger and the mercy of God cannot live in the same divine heart. God's anger is most definitely *never* separated from his love, just as our anger is virtually *always* connected with our self-love. But, does it not help us to face our own anger if we know that God, our Maker and Redeemer, also "gets angry"? Perhaps one of the reasons that we find anger to be such an unacceptable emotion is that our view of God himself, and of his Son, is incomplete.

If, as the Bible tells us, we have been made in the image and likeness of God (Genesis 1:27), then the entire range of human emotions must, in some way, reflect the very character of God. They are broken and blurred reflections, to be sure, but to deny any of them is to repudiate one possible connection that we have with our Creator. Even our anger must remain open and available for God to remake and to use for his own glory. Jesus' harsh treatment of the greedy merchants in the temple tells us that there is divine purpose to the anger that is set against evil and injustice. God's anger is against all that destroys, warps, or abuses his people, whom he made in free, untrammeled love. As imperfect as our own expression of such indignation might be, it is no reason to deny or stifle it. The gospel does not instruct us to become repressed, artificially "good" people. At times we may even have some of God's righteous wrath within us!

At any rate, we do not need to be afraid of feeling. Emotions—all emotions—are an integral part of our created nature. What we should fear, however, is to be blind to whatever is true, about God or about ourselves. And anger is something that is "true" about us both. The issue is not whether or not we get angry (we all do); the issue is whether or not our anger has, as its source, the love of God or the love of ourselves. Being a disciple of Jesus Christ means that we are on the road to learning the difference.

R E F L E C T | *Which is more familiar to you—the idea that God is loving or that God is angry? Why? How does this influence the way that you view yourself or the choices that you make about what to do with your own feelings?*

Day 3   How Much Anger Lives in Your Heart?

READ | Colossians 3:1–17

But now, put them all away: anger, wrath, malice, slander, and foul talk from your mouth. (v. 8)

This week we are reflecting on one of those common and quite understandable human emotions that can, nevertheless, cause us a great deal of difficulty in our relationship with God and with one another. Once we have acknowledged anger's presence in our own hearts—because we have heard its expression from our own lips—how are we to deal honestly with it? Several generations ago, a famous pastor preached a sermon entitled "The Expulsive Power of a Great Affection." Using biblical examples, he argued that when a believer is possessed by a great love for God, that love expels from the heart all negative and harmful things. The pure of heart are those whose hearts are filled to capacity with only one thing— love for God and neighbor. There is no more room in such a heart for anything else. Love has expelled it all.

This is a wonderful concept, to be sure, and opening our hearts to this kind of miraculous makeover is exactly what the life of discipleship is about. But this holy transformation takes place within very ordinary circumstances and among very ordinary fellow sinners. The desire to have our hearts renewed—filled with love—grows and strengthens because we experience how *unloving* we are to the people with whom we live and work and pray each day. This is the world in which we learn love.

Paul points out to the Christians of Colossae some of the things that they allow to occupy space in their hearts and crowd out the Spirit of God. Among those unwelcome (but often entertained) inhabitants is anger and all of its nasty children: malicious feelings, slanderous talk, resentment, impatience, lying, and unforgiveness. These are all indisputable signs that love does not yet fill every room in the house.

Once again, it is for this reason that honestly facing our anger is so imperative. The prophet Jeremiah said that "the heart is deceitful above all things, and desperately corrupt; who can understand it?" (Jeremiah 17:9). Our most inward desires and motivations are usually hid from our own sight, especially when they are entirely opposed to what we know God intends for our lives. How are we to know what lives in us, therefore, if we do not listen carefully to what comes out of us? Our angry reactions to others are among the outward signals that there is something amiss in our lives, that love is lacking and that faith is weak.

REFLECT | *What kinds of circumstances or people most often make you angry? Why? What practical step is God asking of you in order to make more room in your own heart for love?*

Day 4   The Anger of Man

READ | James 1:19–27
For the anger of man does not work the righteousness of God. (v. 20)

There are two important points about anger in this reading from the Letter of James. The first is that, as forceful as anger may be, we actually do have some control over it.

Everyone, says James, must be "slow to anger." There exists a space of time between the cause and the expression of anger, and that space should not be too short. There are times when we are consciously aware of that brief moment of choice, when the initial feelings of anger begin to arise, and we can either take them to God or give vent to them upon others. With practice, the apostle seems to be saying, we can enlarge that moment. We can choose not to fly off the handle.

For some of us, this is a much harder battle than for others. Anger is such a powerful and unpredictable emotion that some of us deny its existence even while others of us give free reign to its destructive forces. François Fénelon, a French archbishop of the late seventeenth century, gave this sage advice through one of his letters: "A heated imagination, vehement feeling, a world of argument, and a flow of words are really useless. The practical thing is to act in a spirit of detachment, doing what one can by God's light, and being content with such success as he gives" (*The Royal Way of the Cross*, p. 133). This is what James is talking about when he counsels us to be slow to anger.

When he writes that heated arguments and violent emotion are "really useless," Fénelon's counsel is also touching upon the second important feature of these verses from James—anger rarely accomplishes the goal for which we aim, nor solves the problem that lies before us. For a brief moment, anger may give us the illusion that we are in control of a certain situation; it may give us a sense of strength and confidence, and it may even intimidate others into doing as we wish, but the long-term result is really nil. "The anger of man," writes James, "does not work [read "accomplish"] the righteousness of God." There is a divine anger that can accomplish divine purposes—consider Jesus chasing the money changers from the temple (as we read from John), or the judgment of God against sin and death (as we will read in Jonah). But rarely is human anger so selflessly motivated or constructively expressed. Through our anger we are usually attempting to control unwelcome circumstances or to shape the attitudes and actions of others to our own liking—in other words, our aim is to get our own way. The anger of man has little to do with love, and far more to do with power.

James gives an interesting piece of his own advice about how such anger might be averted in the first place: "Let every man be quick to hear." There is that compelling charge again—*listen.* Love demands that we be more ready to listen to the other, than to make the other listen to us; and that we listen more intensely to the other's voice than to the demanding cries of our own anger and hurt and fear. For, in the end, anger is usually the heavy instrument of pride, and pride always says, "Listen to *me.*" Listening to the other person, therefore, is sometimes the most practical and effective way of making pride put down its weapons.

R E F L E C T | *Think about a recent example of your own anger—what is it that you were trying to accomplish? If it was against another person, what were you trying to get them to do? What makes it so difficult for you to listen when you are angry?*

Day 5   Do You Do Well to be Angry?

READ | Jonah 4

But it displeased Jonah exceedingly, and he was angry. (v. 1)

Since we have introduced the connection between anger and getting our own way—a connection, by the way, that most of us successfully made at a very, very young age!—let us consider a colorful illustration. Jonah is a delightful and thoroughly human biblical figure. In spite of his flaws, or, more likely, because of them, we feel a genuine kinship with this rebellious and angry character. We know, perhaps, the lengths to which *we* are willing to go in order to avoid those unwelcome tasks that we find so thoroughly disagreeable.

The prophet Jonah took what seemed an effective means of escape in order to avoid the unpleasant mission of proclaiming God's judgment upon Nineveh. It was not that he minded Nineveh's destruction. On the contrary, he would welcome it. He simply did not want to be the one who had to announce the city's terrible fate to its citizens. Most of us are familiar with the story—he tried to flee from God by taking a ship to Tarshish (it is not clear why Jonah thought that God would not be in Tarshish!); during a storm, he was thrown into the sea by the ship's crew; God sent a mighty fish to swallow him and bring him back to shore; there, God gave him his assignment once again and, this time, Jonah consented. The part we are less familiar with is what happened *after* Jonah announced to Nineveh that it was about to be destroyed—the people believed him; they repented and changed their ways; and God withdrew his judgment. Now Jonah really thought he had something to be angry about! He had walked about the city proclaiming its destruction and, instead blessing came. Embarrassed and disappointed, Jonah went off to a corner to sulk. "I knew this would happen," he angrily complained.

Chapter four of this remarkable book is a gem, because it shows a man at his petty worst in conversation (honest conversation, we might add) with his Creator. The remarkable thing is that God took no offense at Jonah's antics. Instead, he engaged his prophet in a reasonable conversation, like a patient father to his stubborn son, in order to make him see the foolishness of his ways. Jonah's anger, truthfully displayed, became God's opportunity to show forth his mercy and to teach his child a lasting lesson of faith.

A thorough reading of the prophets (and of the psalms, as well) will reveal many of these kinds of honest conversations—even arguments—between God and his servants. The key to having the argument settled is found, first, in our willingness to be completely honest, and then, in our willingness to listen. There are some people who maintain a constant grudge against God, who have grown comfortable in their anger against him for any number of reasons. The stories of Jonah and of these other men and women of faith tell us that God understands such intense feelings, and is always ready to listen to them. But such stories also tell us that we, too, may have some listening to do in order to see our anger for what it really is. Opening our hearts to God means handing him our most ugly feelings as well as our most beautiful. Becoming convinced that God is right and that we are wrong can be one of the most delightful and liberating experiences of the Christian life.

REFLECT | *Where do you recognize yourself in the story of Jonah? What "argument" are you having with God these days? What anger do you have against him that you have not yet told him or that has not yet been resolved?*

Day 6   Anger's Fearful Roots

READ | Isaiah 31:1–9

Woe to those who go down to Egypt for help and rely on horses who trust in chariots because they are many and in horsemen because they are very strong. (v. 1)

Let me tell you a story. Today I walked my dog around the block and through the woods just as I usually do each day. She is familiar with every turn, every tree, every lawn, and every person she meets along the way. The route we take is through "her" world, and she always walks it with the carefree spirit of a soul that is altogether at peace with her surroundings. At least, most of the time. Today we were nearing the end of our walk when we turned a corner and met something, someone, utterly unfamiliar. It was actually a person she knew quite well, but today this person was hunched over a wheelbarrow, digging out some dirt with a small shovel that scraped menacingly against the sides of the old metal box.

The dog reacted instantly. She stopped dead in her tracks, spread her legs, lowered her head, raised her fur and began to bark at the top of her lungs. For a few moments there was nothing either of us could do to make her stop. No amount of scolding or soothing, no amount of calling her by name or trying to distract her attention, was able to calm her down. For those moments, until she finally recognized her friend—and, with tail wagging, ran to get a hug—she was wholly given over to her fear, and to the fury that arose from it.

We said earlier that anger is very often a helpful signal that something is amiss in our hearts. For this reason, we need to pay attention when we feel angry, because our reactions may be telling us something more. The saying goes that "the best defense is a good offense," which goes a long way toward explaining that altogether human (and animal) connection between fear and anger. Oft times, our most angry reactions, especially those sudden and unreasonable outbursts that take us (and others) by surprise, are nothing more than the burning flares we send up when we are in trouble.

The prophet is rebuking God's people because, in the fear of their enemies, they are turning for help to the strength of flesh—in this case, to Egypt and its seemingly invincible army—rather than to the Lord. Anger is among those "horsemen of Egypt" that makes us think we are strong and invincible when what we really feel is weak and defenseless. In the hope of safety we lay hold of anger, but such times as these are meant to point us to the only source of reliable help that we have, the Lord of hosts. Sometimes the answer to our angry feelings is to trust the Lord with our own well-being, and the well-being of those whom we love. No other power is sufficient, and especially not the imaginary power that arises out of our own anger. "Impotent rage," is what a friend called it once; it barks loudly and makes a big display, but all the time its heart is racing and it is shaking in its boots.

REFLECT | *What connection do you make between the things that make you angriest and the things that make you fearful? Describe a specific example. In what areas of your life do you have the most difficulty trusting God?*

Day 7   Sharp Contention!

READ | Acts 15:22–41

And there arose a sharp contention, so that they separated from each other; Barnabas took Mark with him and sailed away to Cyprus, but Paul chose Silas and departed, being commended by the brethren to the grace of the Lord. (vv. 39–40)

Anyone who argues that the early church was always harmonious and unified has not read the entire New Testament. In fact, we read of controversy even in the lives of the twelve original disciples. It is a sad, but no less authentic, fact of human relationships that from time to time we are hurt with one another and we get angry, and that from time to time, we may actually turn our backs on one another. In the case of Paul and Barnabas, these two pillars of the church, their dispute over the fitness of John (called Mark) as a missionary companion led them to go their separate ways. Apparently the young and inexperienced Mark had abandoned the team once already (vv. 37–38), and Paul was not willing to trust him on their next journey. Barnabas, on the other hand, was prepared to give Mark another chance. One can see both sides of the argument (which also makes one wonder if God did not use the anger of these two men in order to actually advance the gospel—for now there were two teams instead of one!).

The letters of Paul reveal a man of obvious fiery disposition and single-minded focus, while the Acts of the Apostles portrays Barnabas as a man of great generosity and thoughtfulness. Even the new name given him by the apostles means "son of encouragement" (see Acts 4:36–7). So, the new church of Christ is being served by two men with very different personalities and very different opinions about the best course of action to be taken. Should there not be room in the Body of Christ for both?

Though it is never made explicit, it would seem that Paul and Barnabas eventually reconciled. At least we know from Paul's second letter to Timothy that he not only came to accept Mark, but also to recommend him for his faithful service (4:11). Among the lessons to be drawn from the Bible's forthright presentation of this "sharp contention" is that conflict *does* happen in the Body of Christ and that it can also be resolved.

Paul and Barnabas' argument appears to have been quite volatile. One can only imagine how angry the words must have been in order to turn these two friends and co-workers away from one another. Nevertheless, the things we have discussed this week remind us that such enmity can only be resolved if it is faced directly. Yes, above all we are to love one another. But, as Paul writes to the Romans, love must be "genuine" (12:9). Love for God and neighbor cannot be faked. Its strength and endurance are dependent upon the honesty with which we face those things that would weaken or destroy it. Genuine love comes at a cost.

REFLECT | *How are you facing your real feelings about someone with whom you differ? How can you allow God to help you to resolve those feelings?*

Week Seven Woe Is Me: The Crushing Weight Of Self-Pity

Day 1   Whose Arms are Strong Enough?

R E A D | Isaiah 53

He was despised and rejected by men; a man of sorrows and acquainted with grief. . . . Surely he has borne our griefs and carried our sorrows. (vv. 3, 4)

"I've tripped up and fallen so many times, I just don't know if I can keep at this. Obviously I'm no good at it. I don't think I've got what it takes. It's all just too much for me." Halfway through these twelve weeks it would be surprising indeed if these words, in some form or another, have not already passed through your lips (or, at least through your mind) many times already. Sometimes the journey of the disciple of Christ seems endlessly uphill. Rather than our step growing lighter and quicker, our clumsy feet seem to find absolutely every pothole and every stone along the way. "This is abundant life?" we ask. "This is where following Jesus gets me?"

Failure—there is not a one of us who has not known its bitter taste or been bruised by its heavy stroke. It is a most unwelcome guest for, when it comes into our homes, it usually brings its gloomy companions, disappointment and discouragement. The question before us this week is not about whether or not failure will come through our door. Failure will visit often. He is the first cousin to our fallen human condition and he will always know our address. The question is, how long will we entertain its nasty cohorts? How long will we live with discouragement and entertain despondency? How long will we let them sit at our table?

This week, at the mid-point of these reflections, we turn to the subject of self-pity. We do this, keeping in mind that, like any other sin (and, so long as it diverts us from love for God and for others, it is, most definitely, sin), it need not, it *cannot*, have the last word in our lives. The griefs that pierce our hearts, due either to those circumstances quite beyond our control or to those of our own making, are intimately known to God. He knows better than we, that we are not strong enough to bear them alone. Remember the story of Adam and Eve; God never intended them to "go it alone." They were created to be dependent upon their Maker. Only by their own misguided choices did they and their children come to believe that everything depended upon them.

Some people seem to have a natural penchant for hopefulness and trust. For most of us, however, these are qualities that must be learned, and those lessons begin by returning to the most basic truth of all—God loves us. We have a Savior, One whose arms are more than strong enough to lift us, together with all the sorrows and disappointments that sit heavily upon our own shoulders. Jesus is both the Lamb, who knows the roughness of the journey, as well as the Good Shepherd, who is never far from our bleating cries. Refusing to give in to the insidious temptation that we are "on our own" is the beginning of learning hope. Looking to the love of God rather than to our own unloveliness is the beginning of learning faith. Relying upon the help of God rather than upon our own feeble efforts is the beginning of learning joy.

REFLECT | *Name specifically those places in your life where you are discouraged this week. Now consider the ways in which you can (must) look to God for his help in these places. What is it that you most hope for in your life? What are the ways in which God is answering that desire?*

Day 2   Repentance or Self-pity?

READ | 2 Corinthians 7:2–10

For godly grief produces a repentance that leads to salvation and brings no regret, but worldly grief produces death. (v. 10)

Before we delve further into our discussion of self-pity, we do well to make an important distinction about its meaning. Paul's words to the Christians in Corinth may be helpful.

The apostle knew a good deal about the comfort of God, because he also knew a good deal about affliction and failure. We know that in his service of the gospel, Paul endured many trials and many hardships. Later in this letter, he offered a fairly thorough list to his readers (see 11:23–29). Through these events, Paul learned again and again the priceless lessons of perseverance and hope. God had been his comforter, sometimes through the hearts and hands of his companions, sometimes in the midst of his darkest and most lonely hours. Paul also knew the comfort of God's forgiving love. The conviction that cut into his heart on that day when he met Christ on the road to Damascus (Acts 9:1–19) caused him a burning sorrow that he would remember and speak of for the rest of his life. His face-to-face encounter with

Jesus caused him a painful grief before it brought him to an enduring joy. For this reason, he understood well what the Corinthians were feeling.

In this letter Paul refers to an earlier letter by which he had severely reprimanded the church in Corinth for some serious sin. Titus brings word to Paul, while he is working in Macedonia, that the letter was received, that it caused a good deal of distress and sorrow, but that it also resulted in the Corinthians' repentance followed by a renewed zeal for the gospel. This, writes Paul, is the *"godly grief* that produces repentance that leads to salvation"* (v. 10).

There is a vast difference, says Paul, between "godly grief" and "worldly grief," and that difference is seen most clearly in their exceedingly different results—the first brings salvation while the latter brings death! By "godly grief" Paul is apparently describing repentance, the same response to the conviction of the Holy Spirit that he himself experienced at his conversion. It is "godly" because Paul allowed it to actually open his heart to the love of God and make him responsive to the truth of the gospel. The end result was Paul's salvation, and all the joyful benefits that came with it.

Apparently, something similar happened with the Corinthians. The apostle's message had cut them to the quick, but the grief it caused compelled them only to change their ways and to renew their zeal for God. By "worldly grief," however, Paul means something entirely different, for the world knows only how to help itself, and when its own help fails, there is nowhere else to look for comfort. This is a sadness that actually turns us away from God, closes our hearts to his love, and leaves us alone with our remorse. There is nothing at all "godly" about such grief.

Pain will always compel us to look for relief. The question will always be: to whom will we look? "Godly grief" produces repentance—it draws our vision away from ourselves, toward the only Savior who is able to save. "Worldly grief" produces regret—it drags our vision inward, where we look in vain for the help we need and despair at our lack of it. The fruit of the first is joy. The fruit of the second is self-pity.

REFLECT | *In what area(s) of your life are you now experiencing repentance? In what area(s) are you experiencing remorse? How do you know the difference?*

Day 3   Lord, Where Have You Gone?

READ | Psalm 77

Has [the Lord's] steadfast love forever ceased? Are his promises at an end for all time? Has God forgotten to be gracious? (vv. 8–9)

So, what are some of the signs of self-pity, and what are some of the tools we can use in order to come free of its stifling grip? Recognizing that self-pity has us by the throat is certainly the first step toward getting loose. Then there are some other steps we can take to keep it at bay. For some insight, we turn first to the psalms.

One early pastor of the church compared the book of psalms to a garden wherein one can find growing every possible variety of human emotion: love, hate, anger, fear, joy, praise, hope, sorrow, and self-pity, among others. Another said that the psalms are like mirrors—we can look into any one of them, and, at any given time, we can see our own emotions looking back at us. For example, there is a whole category of psalms that have been called "psalms of lament," and this is one of them. It is easy to see why. Do you "see yourself" in any one of the psalmist's complaints: things are so painful that I have nothing to say; I can't get any sleep; when I think about God I only feel worse; where is God, anyway; has he forgotten all about me; I used to know that God loved me, but not any more; I'm trying my best, but it's just no good?

By the time he "cries aloud," this poet's self-pity has ripened into a full-grown case of hopelessness and accusation against the goodness and mercy of God. As with any of us in such a state, this soul is in danger of losing all desire to be faithful and all determination to be obedient to God and to his will. Self-pity saps the heart of all energy when it convinces it to believe the worst lie of all—that God doesn't care and that, in fact, he never has.

The psalmist makes no attempt to hide or to diminish the depth of his lamentation. In fact, the reason we have it recorded in the Bible in the first place is that the writer presents it as a genuine prayer of the heart. Bringing our true feelings to God is actually the first step toward sorting them all out. The safest place for us to laugh or cry, to grieve or rejoice, even to rant and rave, is before the face of God. "Look at me and tell me what you are feeling," seems to be God's constant invitation to his sons and daughters. Doing so, even in anger, is one way that we begin to turn our eyes heavenward.

Reading the entire psalm reveals to us that there is also a second step toward our recovery. Having poured out all his grievances, the psalmist appears to stop and remind himself that they do not tell the *whole* story of his relationship with God. "I will call to mind the deeds of the Lord," he says. "I will remember thy wonders of old. I will meditate on all thy work and muse on thy mighty deeds" (vv. 11–12). Having gathered all the thorns that he could possibly find in this garden of despair, the psalmist now starts picking some fragrant flowers, and their sweet scent begins to renew his hope. Remembering the things that God has done for us in the past is a most effective way to fight present despondency. The pathway of our lives is plentifully covered with commemorative signs of God's faithfulness, and no amount of grief today can remove these marks of God's lovingkindness.

REFLECT | *If God were actually sitting in a seat across from you, what would you most want to say to him today? Recount for yourself at least six good things that God has done in your life in the last year; in the last week; in the last day.*

Day 4   Child, What Are You Doing Here?

READ | 1 Kings 19:1–18
And there he came to a cave, and lodged there; and behold, the word of the Lord came to him, and said to him, "What are you doing here, Elijah?" (v. 9)

We know the prophet Elijah to be one of God's most faithful servants and zealous defenders. Many of the stories we read of him are filled with intense activity and drama, and it seems in keeping with the rest of his colorful life that, at

its close, he should be taken to heaven in a fiery whirlwind!
(2 Kings 2:11–12). But, did you know that this great man of
faith and courage was also given to bouts of discouragement
and despair? Today's reading, from the history of Israel's
monarchy, describes Elijah in his most dispirited condition,
and it does so with a bit of humor as well.

The end of the previous chapter left Elijah enjoying
the sweet taste of victory over the pagan prophets of Baal
(see 18:17–46). Before the eyes of all his enemies, God had
vindicated Elijah by answering his prayer: first, he sent fire
from heaven to consume a thoroughly waterlogged offering,
and then he sent rain to end a long season of drought. In
every way, Elijah was shown to be a true prophet, and this
only raised the ire of his most bitter enemy, Jezebel the
queen. This is where we pick up the story.

Elijah quickly abandons faith for fear when he hears
the threats of the queen. Having just stared down an entire
nation, what does this man of faith do in the face of Jezebel's
fumings? He runs away. Into the wilderness he flees, and
there, discouraged and full of self-pity, he simply gives up:
"That's enough. Now, Lord, just take away my life" (v. 4).
God does no such thing, however. Instead, he feeds him and
sends him on his way.

Elijah's next step is a cave, far off in Horeb. But in this
place, before he can say anything at all, God puts to him
this question: "What are you doing here, Elijah?" The rest
of the story tells us that Elijah really has no good answer.
Thinking that he has been abandoned ("I, even only I am
left," v. 10), Elijah discovers that there are thousands of
others who are keeping faith with God (v. 18). With a "still,
small voice," God quiets Elijah's complaints and calms his

trembling heart. Reassuring Elijah that the cause is not lost, God sends him back to Israel to finish his work.

The wilderness and the cave—are these not apt images for a "place" we might call self-pity? One is dry, the other is dark; one is expansively large and dangerous, the other is oppressively small and confining; in one it seems you cannot hear the sound of your own voice, while in the other it seems your own voice is all that you can hear. In both of these dreary places, God comes to us. We may run to them when we are afraid and discouraged, but we can be certain that God will get there first. "Child, what are you doing here?" he will ask. And our answers will make no more sense than did Elijah's.

Remember that kind and probing question the next time you find yourself feeling downcast, defeated, or sorry for yourself. Answer it as best you can, and then listen for what God will say to you. "Go, return," was God's message to Elijah. God still had much that he intended to do through his faithful servant, and others were still waiting to benefit from his work. So Elijah "departed from there" (v. 19), and returned.

REFLECT | *To what places do you run to "hide" when you are feeling sorry for yourself? What are you doing there? Notice how Elijah's discouragement followed immediately on the heels of his success. What lessons can you draw from this?*

Day 5　Lord, Don't You Care?

READ | Luke 10:38–42

Lord, do you not care that my sister has left me to serve alone?
(v. 40)

Mary and Martha and their brother, Lazarus, were friends as well as followers of Jesus. The Gospel of John tells us, "Now Jesus loved Martha and her sister and Lazarus" (11:5), and, from the tears that Jesus shed at Lazarus' tomb and in the presence of Mary and Martha, we can infer that Jesus held these friends dear in his heart. So it must always have been a joy for these three to host Jesus in their home, and it would appear that they did so more than once. The first occasion, however, seems to be this one recorded in Luke's Gospel.

No doubt, when Jesus came, others came with him. All of the twelve? Quite likely. In any case, there was enough work to do that "Martha was distracted with much serving." You can imagine the scene, can you not? Jesus and the disciples are gathered at the table. Lazarus is asking questions of this young and fascinating rabbi, because he has already received news about some of his wise words and miraculous deeds. Mary, who may have brought the water so that these weary travelers could wash their feet, stands politely at the entry to the room. Before long, however, she forgets her other duties and gradually begins to move closer. Every word of Jesus' seems to draw her. She ends up sitting at his feet.

Meanwhile, Martha is at work preparing the meal. After all, it seems that she is the one who has invited all the guests. She awaits Mary's return so that they can share the duties, but her sister never comes. A bit of irritation grows to genuine annoyance when, looking into the room, she realizes that Mary has no intention of returning to the kitchen. Martha is on her own to do all the work. She returns to the kitchen, but all the time her troubled feelings are churning: "This isn't right; this isn't fair. Why should I have to do all the work? Why isn't my sister helping me? Even the rabbi would agree with me." So she turns, and makes her appeal for him to correct her sister. And, in doing so, Martha is led to break all the rules of proper etiquette by complaining to her guest about how much *she* had to do to feed him! This story is a high-definition picture of the dance of jealousy and self-pity.

The answer to Martha's (and our) predicament is actually presented in the story itself—"one thing is needful" (v. 42). The eyes of self-pity are prone to wander about the rooms of our lives and fix upon anyone else who seems to have it better than we do. Self-pity whispers: "This isn't right; this isn't fair. Why should I have it so hard? Why should she have it so good? Even God would agree with me." You and I know this to be true, because we have heard this whispering voice ourselves, and we have agreed with it. All the time we are having this sort of conversation with ourselves, however, the Lord, who himself is the "one thing needful," waits for our wandering eyes to make their way toward him. Fixing the eyes of our hearts upon Jesus is the only lasting remedy for the kind of feeling sorry for ourselves that springs from jealousy. Everything else can be taken away from us (v. 42).

REFLECT | *What unfair duties or responsibilities do you bear that sometimes (all the time?) cause you to feel sorry for yourself?*

What is the "good portion" that Jesus is inviting you to receive from his hand today? When you feel sorry for yourself, what are the specific ways in which you can turn your eyes to Jesus?

Day 6   A Hope That Lifts the Soul

READ | Psalm 42

Why are you cast down, O my soul, and why are you disquieted within me? Hope in God; for I shall again praise him, my help and my God. (v. 5)

Alexander Maclaren, the great nineteenth-century English Baptist preacher, says about Psalm 42, "The whole psalm reads like the sob of a wounded heart. The writer of it is shut out from the Temple of his God, from the holy soil of his native land. One can see him sitting solitary yonder in the lonely wilderness . . . with a longing, wistful gaze, yearning across the narrow valley and the rushing stream that lay between him and the land of God's chosen people, and his eye resting perhaps on the mountain top that looked down upon Jerusalem. . . . He was depressed because he was shut out from the tokens of God's presence [the Temple]; and *because he was depressed, he shut himself out from the reality of the Presence*" (Alexander Maclaren, *Psalms for Sighs*, italics mine).

Maclaren makes an interesting point. On the one hand, it is quite understandable that the psalmist should be "cast down" under the burden of his sad circumstances. He could remember the days when he made his way to Jerusalem and the beautiful temple of the Lord with singing and dancing.

Now, separated from the home he loved, he felt like a deer without water, and his soul languished. On the other hand, *because* he languished, he turned his face from God, and, for a time, he shut the gates of his own heart to God's entry.

Have you noticed this insidious thing about the fiend called self-pity? it provokes us to do the very thing that will keep it nourished and strong. We *feel* that God is not present, or that God does not love us, or that we are too pitiful to be loved. The strength of these feelings convinces us that what they are saying is true. So we end up turning away from God, and our hearts become even more discouraged. The psalmist's prayer provides an escape from this vicious circle: "My soul is cast down within me, *therefore* I remember thee" (v. 5). Wise to self-pity's sneaky ways, he gives his heart a good talking-to: "Listen, my heart. What are you doing down there? The things that you are telling me are just not true. God is not like that. You are telling me that he does not love me, but I know better."

An older and wiser friend met me on the road once, when I was in a particularly bad way. Discouraged and lost, I told him that I was confessing to God repeatedly how faithless and fearful I felt. But it seemed all for naught, and I was tiring of it. "Have you talked with God recently about the things he has done for you?" asked my friend. My silence was answer enough. "Because," he said thoughtfully, "I think one act of thanking God for his goodness is worth more than a dozen confessions of your own sin." I don't know how the theologians would parse that sentence, but I do know that encounter started my own journey back to the face of God. Like the psalmist, I found solace and then joy by "remembering" God.

REFLECT | *What has God done for you in the last week? Name the places where he is present in your life, and in the lives of those you love. What do you need to say to your own soul today to help it turn its eyes toward heaven?*

Day 7　Go Forward!

READ | Exodus 14:5–31

Fear not, stand firm, and see the salvation of the Lord, which he will work for you today. (v. 13)

One final thing must be said about this week's subject—sometimes feeling sorry for ourselves is the understandable, if unfortunate, result of being faced with circumstances quite beyond our own control. Sometimes, the "overwhelming odds" of life's pressures simply get us down. The endless tasks of caring for home and family, the demands of the job, conflicts with those we love most, financial strains and worries for the future—these sometimes swell up like a stormy sea and overcome us with their billowing waves. We understand the plight of the lonely Breton fisherman who prayed: "Lord, be good to me; the sea is so wide, and my boat is so small."

The story of God's deliverance of the people of Israel has, for centuries, been a source of consolation and promise. (In some Christian traditions, the account is read on the eve of every Easter, reminding the listener that, when he divided the Red Sea, God was just getting warmed up to open the Garden Tomb.) The people's hope for a clean escape from slavery was distinctly thwarted as Pharaoh's army charged them from behind and the sea loomed up ahead. And, from within, there arose the worst enemy of all: Fear, panic, self-pity, accusation, and anger—the whole discouraging gang got together to make its malicious attack. "We should have stayed in Egypt," the people cried. "What are *you* doing to us, Moses, and what were we thinking to have ever followed you?" I'm sure we all know the desperate tone in their voices.

We also know how the story ends, but how *did* the people get from one side to the other? "Go forward," God told them through the mouth of Moses. As hopelessly impossible as the situation appears, go forward. The Lord will do the fighting, while you turn your face forward. The Lord will make a way, while you take another trembling step forward. The Lord will work for you today, while you work to set your sight forward.

Only after they had completed their journey across the sea did the children of Israel get the full view of what had happened behind them. From the far shore they could now see all the signs of God's deliverance, whereas before, from the midst of their troubles, all they could see were the signs of their own impending doom. And, when they saw the great work that the Lord had done, "they believed in the Lord and in his servant Moses." The tone of their voices was then utterly changed and raised in the praise of their Deliverer. If you have time today, you should read their song in the first half of the next chapter of Exodus, where you will find these words: "Thou hast led in thy steadfast love the people whom thou hast redeemed, thou hast guided them by thy strength to thy holy abode." How did the people get from one side to the other?—God led them . . . and they went forward.

REFLECT | *Where are the voices coming from that are telling you to give up? What are they saying? Where are the voices coming from that are telling you to keep going forward? What are they saying? Which voices are you going to listen to?*

Week Eight The Irresistible Strength
Of A Forgiving Heart

Day 1   Overcome Evil With Good

R E A D | Romans 12:1–21

Repay no one evil for evil, but take thought for what is noble in the sight of all. (v. 17)

In many respects, Paul's letter to the Romans is his most theological work. Through the first eleven chapters he sets forth both a reasonable as well as a passionate argument for faith in Jesus Christ. He traces God's work through creation and in the covenant with Abraham and the people of Israel; he demonstrates the character of belief in God's promises, and makes the case that all those promises have been fulfilled in Christ; he explains the overwhelming power of sin and describes its defeat under the even more overwhelming power of the Cross. "O the depth of the riches and wisdom and knowledge of God!" Paul concludes. "To him be glory for ever. Amen" (11:33, 36). With that exclamation, he begins to apply the things we believe to the ways that we live. *Therefore*, he says, given all the strength and beauty of God's mercies, you can be living lives of strength and beauty yourselves (12:1–2). For the remaining four chapters of his letter, his words are decidedly pointed and practical, and, not surprisingly, he opens by making the case for loving one another.

God's love, as we know, takes very concrete forms ("the Word became *flesh*")—it has far less to do with our feelings than with our actions. Perhaps in no case is this more evident than in that internal conflict we all know between the need to forgive and the desire for revenge. The cliché goes: "Don't get mad—get even!" We human beings have an uncanny ability to tenaciously remember wrongs that have been done to us. Often the heated conflicts that arise between wives and husbands, or among children, or with friends, are actually stoked by the embers of hurts that we have quietly, steadily, and sometimes quite unconsciously fanned over time. When opportunities to "even the score" come along, our supply of wounded feelings and angry reactions is at the ready, and we fling out our vengeful thoughts from it like so many hot sparks fly from the fire. What's more, our vindictiveness comes in a whole range of shapes and sizes: angry words, humorous remarks, hurtful actions, lapses of memory, and stubborn refusals, just to name a few. What is more, we sometimes visit these reactions upon innocent bystanders who just happen to "walk into our path." Something they say or do hits a nerve in us and brings down upon their own blameless heads the vengeance that we were really saving for someone else.

The apostle Paul writes that the only "burning coals" we should be heaping on anyone's head should be deeds of love and mercy (v. 20). He says that true nobility of heart is found in forgiveness rather than in reprisal, and that the truly strong are those who overcome evil before they are overcome by it. In the end, he says, only God is in a position to justly vindicate the aggrieved or persecuted soul, because God is the only one who is just in the first place. Putting our own hand to vengeance is not only contrary to the law of love, but it usurps the place of God himself.

This week, we will reflect further on what the Scriptures teach us about the destructive power of human vindictiveness, and how it is overcome by the healing power of divine love.

REFLECT | *Think about the events of the past week. Even if you did not act upon them, what desires did you have to "get even" with someone? When you do act upon them (in thought or in deed), what different shapes does your own vindictiveness take?*

Day 2   A Hurt for a Hurt

READ | Matthew 5:38–48

But I say to you, Love your enemies and pray for those who persecute you, so that you may be sons of your Father who is in heaven. (vv. 44–45)

Most of us wholly consent to the ideal of total love for absolutely everyone, including our enemies. We believe this to be a basic Christian principle that is in every way consistent with the gospel. But the ideal quickly succumbs to the severe blow of a real offense—a real harmful word, a real slight, or a real attack. The loud crack made by some concrete hostility thrown against us drowns out the sound of all our good intentions. Then, our hurt feelings scream out, pushing aside all our convictions with their shrill demands to be avenged. Is love for our enemies really possible?

Let us first agree that, as impossible as these instructions may seem (and this could be said for the entire Sermon on the Mount), Jesus does not waste his breath giving directions that cannot somehow be followed. In fact, "directions" may be a helpful way to look at what Jesus is teaching, for directions are designed to successfully guide us from one place to another. How do we move, in this case over some fairly rocky and uneven ground, from our starting point—

seeking revenge—to our destination—love? And what are the turns we have to make along the way?

We can begin with the realization that you and I were once God's enemies and that the way he "won us over" to his side was with love. The Bible says that, while we were *still* enemies, while we were *yet* sinners, Christ died for us (see Romans 5:6–11). God did not wait for us to come around before he sent his Son. Love often has to be sent one way before it can ever come the other.

Second, love for one's enemies is not the reason but the sign that we are children of our Father who is in heaven. Our inheritance as children of God is not only the forgiveness of our own sins, but also the God-given ability to forgive the sins of others. By the Holy Spirit's help, it is now a divine trait received from God that we hold in common with our most direct "blood relative"—Jesus himself. Once, when defending the Christian faith, the early church teacher Tertullian fixed upon one distinctive mark. "All people love their friends," he said, "but only Christians love their enemies."

Third, such forgiving love is rarely, if ever, effortless. Love is a very tangible and often difficult series of choices and actions. Among its practical expressions, says Jesus, is prayer—"pray for those who persecute you." By these instructions, Jesus is asking no more of his followers than he would do himself, even while suffering the most evil of offenses against him: "Father, forgive them, for they know not what they do" (Luke 23:34). Long before any sentiments of love may arise in our hearts, our lips can still love when they say, "Father, forgive us our sins as we forgive those who sin against us" (Matthew 6:12).

Someone has said that our enemies can be our greatest teachers, because their actions more quickly unveil some of the secret things that are in our hearts than would ever emerge in the presence of friends. Once those "secret things" do emerge—the hurt, the anger, the vengeful feelings— Jesus gives us directions for how to move from our hearts to his own. It is the way of love.

REFLECT | *Name one "enemy" you have today. What tangible steps of forgiveness and love is God asking you to take? Will you?*

Day 3   Revenge: The Weakest Alternative

READ | Genesis 4:1–16
And if you do not do well, sin is couching at the door; its desire is for you, but you must master it. (v. 7)

In case there was any question about the seriousness of vindictiveness and its consequences, we have the tragic tale of Cain and Abel. The Bible presents their story as almost the immediate aftermath of the "fall" of their parents, Adam and Eve. Whereas God, from the first day of creation, had intended life for his sons and daughters, the terrible result of their rebellion was the complete opposite. They had been warned that death would follow their proud act, so the church has always understood our mortality to be interwoven with our fallen condition. Still, both life and death were to remain in the hands of God. It was for God alone to give, and to take away. What is uniquely horrific about the story of Cain and Abel, therefore, is that it is about life and death being seized by the hands of sinful humanity. It is the story of the first murder.

While the events that led to Cain's violent act are somewhat obscure (why did God "have regard" for his brother's offering, but not for his?), the immediate causes are quite clear: Cain became jealous of his brother; that jealousy evolved into bitter anger and resentment; then, when the opportunity presented itself, Cain got his revenge. Of course, he more than evened the score; his deed went far beyond "an eye for an eye." Nevertheless, the principle of revenge is at work. Convinced that Abel had wronged him by taking something that was rightfully his—that is, God's approval—Cain plotted and succeeded in wronging Abel in return, by taking something from him—his life.

Violence, even if it is only acted out in one's imagination, is so often the fruit of vindictive feelings, but it does not have to be. Cain had opportunity to stop the downward spiral of his own thoughts and actions, but, quite simply, he did not choose to do so. In his conversation with Cain, God portrayed sin as being like a beast laying in wait at the door for its victims. It is strong, but it can be mastered.

Like all sin, it takes more strength to *resist* the temptation for revenge than it takes to *give in* to it. This is true of most any act of self-discipline or self-denial, as well. True strength lies in mastering our darker motivations, not in giving unrestrained vent to them. God accepted, and no doubt understood, the fact of Cain's anger and jealousy, but he sternly warned him not to let these monsters consume his better judgment.

Interestingly, the weakling of vindictiveness disguises itself as a means to power. We are tempted to think that, if

We hope you will enjoy this book and find it useful in enriching your life.

Book title: _____

Your comments: _____

How you learned about this book: _____

Why did you buy this book? _____

If purchased: Bookseller _____ City _____ State _____

I would like to know more about: _____

_____

Name _____ Street _____

City _____ State _____ Zip _____

E-mail _____

Phone (_____) _____ Would you like to hear from us by phone? _____

PARACLETE PRESS

PO Box 1568 • Orleans, MA 02653 • 1-800-451-5006 • www.paracletepress.com

PARACLETE PRESS
PO Box 1568
Orleans, MA 02653

we could only get even, we would feel "stronger." We think that whatever has been "taken" from us has left us weak (i.e., we lose an argument), when, in fact, our greatest weakness is our inability to stop the craving to get it back (i.e., to win). For example, how many arguments have you rewound in your mind, so that you could insert just the right word or phrase that would win the day and show your opponent just how shrewd you are? That's vindictiveness at work. Now, try to stop having those imaginary fights. Which is easier?

REFLECT | *What conversations or events are you playing out in your own mind these days? How do phrases like "give in," "let go," and "give up" make you feel? Why? What is the most effective means of "mastering" your vindictiveness?*

Day 4   Who is the Final Winner?

READ | Genesis 39
But the Lord was with Joseph and showed him steadfast love. (v. 21)

Today, we turn to one of the most classic examples of revenge in the Bible. After reading the story of Joseph and Potiphar's wife, no one should think that the Scriptures are anything but candid in their portrayals of twisted values, sexual desire, and vengeful deception. This story has all the drama and intrigue of a soap opera. It also contains an important lesson.

It is, of course, the story of unrequited passion and of the revenge that springs from it.

Vengeance borne of humiliation will always turn attraction into hatred. Consider the effects of something like gossip or backbiting. (Does the fact that we hardly use these words anymore say something about how common they have become?) The angry pain caused by such remarks has been the cause of countless estranged friendships and broken families. With her own proud and lustful advances spurned by Joseph, Potiphar's wife planned her retaliation, and succeeded. It appears that vindictiveness wins the day . . . but only the day. The spotlight moves elsewhere, and from this point on, we hear nothing more of Potiphar's wife. It seems that she only had a bit part to play and on a much bigger stage than she imagined. From the perspective of heaven, she gets away with nothing at all.

Remember that Joseph was already the victim of his brothers' vengeful betrayal. His enslavement in Egypt was already that direct result of jealousy and vindictive scheming (see Genesis 37). But, what his brothers (and Potiphar's wife) had planned for Joseph's undoing, God planned to use for Joseph's making. Following their eventual reconciliation, Joseph said to them, "You meant evil against me; but God meant it for good, to bring it about that many people should be kept alive, as they are today" (Genesis 50:20). The Psalms tell us: "His feet were hurt with fetters, his neck was put in a collar of iron; until what he had said came to pass the word of the LORD tested him" (105:17). From God's perspective, it was "the word of the Lord" that was at work in Joseph, so that even his brothers' cruel and unfair treatment could be transformed into the means for his blessing and maturing.

This is not to say that evil and malice are in any way defensible. There are things that have happened in some of our lives that should never be overlooked or excused. But God is the only just and perfect vindicator, and, though his ways seem dark and slow, he is the Master of bringing good out of evil. And there is no sweeter "revenge" than that. Joseph's enslavement to Potiphar led to his imprisonment, which led to his employment by Pharaoh, which eventually led to the salvation of his entire family and the formation of the Hebrew people. Suppose he had escaped from Egypt and returned to exact his own vengeance upon his brothers. Or, once he was invested with the authority of Pharaoh himself, suppose he had executed his brothers in justifiable retribution for their spitefulness to him.

Aside from the fact that revenge should always be left to God, exacting retribution from another may actually frustrate the deeper purposes of God in our lives. When we reach our hand out to vengeance, we may be deflecting God's hand reaching out to us.

REFLECT | *With what unfair circumstances in your own life is God asking you to trust him? Give an example of at least one event in your own life when God "turned evil into good." Who do you need to forgive today in order not to put your hand to vengeance?*

Day 5　Whose Words Shall Prevail?

READ | Mark 6:7–29

And Herodias had a grudge against [John] and wanted to kill him. (v. 19)

John the Baptist was like the prophet Elijah of old: bold in his dedication to the will of God and fearless in his confrontation with power and corruption. With the single-minded intention of being true to his God, he did not hesitate to call all people—both low and high alike—to account for their actions. His cry for repentance, as he announced the coming of God's kingdom, was heard in the wilderness and in the palace. In John's eyes, God's standards were for *everyone.*

Herod the king had unlawfully married his brother's wife, Herodias, after divorcing his own. Faithful to his own convictions, and heedless of his own safety, John cried out against this, and brought down upon his head the vengeful wrath of Herodias, who, Luke understates, "had a grudge against him and wanted to kill him" (v. 19). As we noted in other readings, and in the life of Jesus himself, the work of a prophet was always dangerous, especially when it required them to speak God's word to those who were more interested in power than in the truth. In such cases, the prophet's only protection was God himself. In John's case, the woman he offended accomplished her plans to silence him, when Herod, drunk and inflated with vanity, promised the sultry Salome whatever she asked, "even half of my kingdom." The kingdom is not what Herodias wanted. It was revenge.

It is helpful to look at these events through two sets of eyes, Herodias' and John's. From Herodias' point of view, John had overstepped himself by addressing criticism against one as important and superior as she. She found his remarks offensive to the extreme.

"What right does he have to speak to me in such a way?" she undoubtedly complained to her husband. Her interest, of course, was not in what was true, but in what was expedient. In other words, anything that would reinforce the manner in which she lived her life was to be welcomed, while whatever called it into question was to be rejected (along with whoever it was that asked the question!).

John, on the other hand, was more interested in truth than in power. He dressed and ate like the poor man that he was and made the wilderness his home. He loved God, and was intensely committed to proclaiming a message that would cut out the diseased growth of Israel and help restore a strong and healthy people of faith. "Repent!" he cried, "The kingdom of heaven is at hand." It was neither an easy nor necessarily a reassuring message to give, but it stirred everyone who heard it: some went to be baptized by him in the Jordan, confessing their sins; others mocked and waited to see him get into trouble.

Herodias' commitment to power made her untruthful, while John's commitment to truth made him powerful. In the end, she took a life, while he gave one. Her act of vengeance was designed to protect her superior image and to maintain her grasp of power. His act of submission was freely given for the sake of God's word, and the only image he needed to protect was but a reflection of that Word. "He must increase, but I must decrease," he once said in reference to Jesus (John 3:30). Herodias sought to prevail over John, and used the means of deceit and revenge in order to do so. John never sought to prevail in anything, but only to be faithful, and the means at hand were love for and obedience to his God. Two perspectives on life were moving two hearts in two extremely different directions. Which way are you going?

REFLECT | *Which way are you going? Which way do you want to go? How will you get there?*

Day 6   A New Commandment

READ | 1 Thessalonians 5

See that none of you repays evil for evil, but always seek to do good to one another and to all. (v. 15)

On the very night of his betrayal and arrest, you remember, Jesus shared a meal with his disciples in the Upper Room (see John 13:1–12). In preparation for supper, in an act of unconditional love and humility, he washed all of the disciples' feet, including Judas'. Knowing full well what was soon to take place, and that the catalyst for all those horrid events would be the hypocritical kiss of his friend, Jesus bent to the ground, poured water on Judas' feet, and dried them with his own hands. Then, after the meal and after Judas had gone out from among them, as if to explain the entire meaning of his life and ministry, he charged the remaining few with these profound words: "A new commandment I give to you, that you love one another;

even as I have loved you, that you also love one another. By this all men will know that you are my disciples, if you have love for one another" (John 13:34–35).

You will pardon the pun if I say that Paul puts feet on this commandment when he writes his letter to the Christians in Thessalonica. As always, his words reveal his uncanny ability to soar to the heavens with his theology, and then plummet to earth with his most practical advice. "See that none of you repays evil for evil, but always seek to do good to one another and to all" (v. 15). There it is again, the same direction he gave to the Christians in Rome (Romans 12:17).

Do you notice that the Bible's instruction is to do more than simply resist the temptation to get even? As difficult as that is, it is only the beginning: it is only the first half of the divine duty with which we have been entrusted. Withholding evil in the face of evil is a start. Doing good in the face of evil is what it means to follow Jesus. In this case the saying is true—the best defense *is* a good offense. The most effective way we fend off the desire for revenge is by feeding the desire to love.

We live in an evil world where people do bad things to other people. They lie and cheat and hurt one another by their words and by their actions. They do evil to one another, and no more vehemently than when evil has been done to them. Sometimes we have been the perpetrators, and sometimes we have been the victims. It all becomes a vicious cycle of wrongdoing if someone does not stop and then turn around and go in the opposite direction. That is what Paul is talking about here. That is what Jesus is demonstrating to his disciples—an entirely different way to live.

Love compels us to run to the cross of Christ when evil is done to us. There, we gaze upon One who when reviled did not revile back; who did not complain to his accusers, but prayed for them; who could have brought down the wrath of heaven upon his tormentors, but instead poured out for them the love of God. How can we stay long at that cross, and still desire to wreak vengeance upon those who, for reasons we do not understand (and which they do not fully understand either), seek to do us harm? We do not have to repay evil with evil. For once we start down that course, what real difference is there between ourselves and those whom we call "evil"? The strength of love is ours to wield at any time, because it was put into our hands by the Lord of love himself. Let those who seek to follow Christ learn his way of love and leave the judgment with God!

REFLECT | *What are the weapons of vengeance that God wants you to put down today? What are the tools of love that he wants you to take up? What "good" thing can you do today for someone who has done you "evil"?*

Day 7   Worthy to Suffer Dishonor

READ | Acts 5:12–42
Then they left the presence of the council, rejoicing that they were counted worthy to suffer dishonor for the Name. (v. 41)

As their penalty for preaching the gospel and healing the sick, the apostles were arrested and thrown into prison. It would not be the last time. On this occasion, they were miraculously released by an angel, and instructed to again stand and teach "the words of this Life" in the temple. Seized a second time, they were carried before the Council where, after declaring that they "must obey God rather than men," they were beaten and charged not to speak in the name of Jesus and released. Twenty-four hours of serving God, doing good, witnessing miracles, and preaching the gospel—in return for which they received a sleepless night, imprisonment, threats of death, beatings, and warnings to stop. What a deal!

There is something noble going on here that appeals to us all. And nothing is nobler than the reaction of these men to their unjust treatment at the hands of others. They returned home, and then returned to their mission, *rejoicing*, not because their enemies had been defeated, not because their honor had been vindicated, and not because hundreds had been converted to faith in Christ that day. They rejoiced because they had been treated just as their Lord had been treated.

As we finish this week's thoughts about our innate, human desire to get even, let this lesson carry our minds and hearts to a higher plane. God's honor is at stake, and some are called to suffer *dis*honor for the sake of serving him. Not everyone. Not even every Christian. But some are called to bear that burden, to carry that part of the cross for the sake of the whole Body of Christ. The apostles counted it an honor. Do we?

Perhaps it would help us to once again accept the reality that following Jesus comes at a price. We cannot expect to be faithful disciples of Christ and to live a pain-free life in this world. For this world is still hostile to the things of

God, and the spirit of this world is antithetical to the spirit of God. Those who follow Jesus *will* suffer some degree, some form of hurt, rejection, and persecution. It may be slight, or it may be severe. What is more, we may visit it, even unintentionally, upon one another. Those, perhaps, are the times when the pain is most bitter. In any case, we have a decision to make about how we will respond to it. This week's reflections have given us an alternative to the vengeful ways that we might choose most naturally. They are a reminder that we can choose the "still more excellent way" of love (1 Corinthians 12:31).

REFLECT | *What is it costing you this week to follow Jesus Christ? How can you turn that "price" into a "prayer" of praise and thanksgiving to God?*

Week Nine When I Fall I Shall Rise

Day 1   Delivered!

READ | Psalm 34

I sought the Lord, and he answered me, and delivered me from all my fears. (v. 4)

David is singing a song of hope and confidence in the Lord, giving joyful testimony to the goodness and power of God, and doing so with every bit as much intensity as we have already encountered in other psalms of grief and complaint. (Remember, the psalms are the prayer book of the human heart, in all its variable conditions!) On this day, he has something very tangible for which to praise his God—God protected and delivered him from the hands of his enemies (see 1 Samuel 21:10–22:1). After days of living in fear for his life, he now enjoyed the fresh taste of freedom and safety once again. This was a new day, and he would praise God for it.

As we travel this remarkable journey of discipleship, we too need days of new beginnings, and they do not need to be as dramatic as David's in order to bring praise to our lips. Any path we pursue in the name of our Lord can become wearisome or troubling over time, especially one that requires discipline and self-denial. Sometimes we slip or stumble along the way, and sometimes we trip over our own wobbly feet, straight into the hands of our old "enemies." We falter, we fall, and we fail. What then?

The prophet Micah, like all the prophets, carried a heavy load of responsibility in the service of God and, from time to time, he fell down under the weight of it. Then it was that he declared: "But as for me, I will look to the Lord,

I will wait for the God of my salvation; my God will hear me. Rejoice not over me, O my enemy; when I fall, I shall rise; when I sit in darkness, the Lord will be a light to me" (Micah 7:7–8). *When* I fall, he said, not *if* I fall. For just such times, what are the psalmist and the prophet telling us to do?

First, remember the Lord's help in the past. When the dark, old "enemies" hover over you, call back to your mind those blessed days you have already enjoyed, when light and hope pierced through the shadow and you knew that God was near at hand. You know that such moments are in your memory somewhere; it's just that you have forgotten them. They are like the seed sown by the roadside that the birds of the air (the frets and cares and demands of the day) came along and plucked away, to keep them from taking root. Remembering God's love is like re-gathering those precious seeds and re-planting them in your heart. They may not make the current troubles disappear, but they will most assuredly give you a different perspective on them. David "blessed the Lord" because the Lord blessed David—he answered, delivered, heard, saved, kept, and redeemed David. This truth could not be denied. Present failings may conceal past victories, but they can never erase them.

Second, forget your failings in the past. Do you remember the apostle Paul's declaration about "forgetting what lies behind and straining forward to what lies ahead"? It was said with the same assurance in God's help that inspired Micah to say confidently, "when I fall, I *shall* rise." This day is a new day. Past failures, mistakes, disobediences belong where you left them—in the past. What is it about this penchant we have for forgetting God's help and remembering our own failings? Today is a day to reverse that perverse routine. "Look to him and be radiant." He has delivered us in the past, and he will free us in this present.

REFLECT | *List at least a half dozen testimonies you have to the love and power of God working on your behalf. Why do you think our own failings come to mind so much more often than God's blessings?*

Day 2   The Source of our Joy

READ | Luke 10:1–20

Nevertheless, do not rejoice in this, that the spirits are subject to you; but rejoice that your names are written in heaven. (v. 20)

This may seem a rather strange story to be discussing at this point on our journey. We are in the midst of some serious work, endeavoring to do something that we believe is both in God's name and in our best interest and, all along, trying to keep our "eyes on the prize." The hope of success (or the fear of failure) is actually one of the things that keeps us going, is it not? Yes, but Jesus is also waving a big caution flag about it.

As desirable and "good" as it is, our view of success is not the same as Jesus' view. In the kingdom of God, success actually is not a compelling enough goal to pursue. Jesus hears the delight of his disciples as they list off all their success stories, but he knows the true nature of success; he knows both its brevity as well as its potential dangers.

We have all witnessed what "success" at its extreme can do to a person. We see it sometimes in public figures when they allow the adulation of the crowd to blind them to the realities of life. Becoming intoxicated by such praise and recognition, they then become addicted to it, and live only for more and more approval. Like any addiction, other than a pure love for God, the blind craving for success has the power to destroy, to take the soul out of a person. This can happen in the realm of spiritual things just as easily as the world of material things. Consider those successful spiritual leaders, for example, who allowed their God-given success to "go to their heads" and plunged forward disastrously to their own ruin and the scandalizing of those who followed them. Today's "successes," like all our works, reminds the psalmist, "pass away like smoke" (Psalm 102:3).

Of course, these are extreme examples and, for most of us, out of our league. But, so too is the example of Jesus and his miracle-working disciples. The principle, however, applies to us all. Jesus is saying that the true object of our rejoicing should never be something as fleeting as success. We can be rightfully grateful for our achievements, and we should be thrilled when we "hit the targets" that have been set before us. But, says Jesus, there is a deeper and more lasting joy to be found elsewhere, and that is not dependent upon what we have done or failed to do. Neither our successes nor our failures are the things that define us and ultimately give our lives meaning.

Having our names written in heaven—inscribed with the indelible ink of Jesus' blood—means that God knows us, and that our true citizenship is in his kingdom. This calls for a rejoicing that can never be dampened or taken away.

Yes, we have been called, as were the first disciples, to do great things for God. But the only lasting source of our joy is the great thing he has done for us. We move on from past and present failures, and we move beyond past and present successes. In the end, all of them are only stepping-stones to our true goal, and He awaits our coming.

REFLECT | *How much does the desire to be "successful" motivate your life? How much does the fear of "failure" motivate your life? How can you come to see both your successes and your failures from God's point of view?*

Day 3   The Poverty of Job

READ | Job 1:1–2:10
Naked I came from my mother's womb, and naked shall I return; the Lord gave, and the Lord has taken away; blessed be the name of the Lord. (1:21)

"There was a man in the land of Uz, whose name was Job"—and thus the sometimes disturbing but always fascinating story of Job begins. He could be anyone, really—anyone who enjoyed the pleasures of family and business, home and friends, anyone who knew enough peace and good health to be content, anyone who endeavored to build a good life for themselves and for their children. Job could also be anyone for whom a single instant of time changed everything. In that "single instant" Job lost his children, his livelihood, and then his health. What he did not lose, however, was his faith, or his God.

This is not to say that Job did not struggle or complain or fight. In fact, the rest of the book of Job is the record of his struggles as heard from his own lips and described by his three so-called "comforters." Job was a man of faith, to be sure, and he confessed that faith when he blessed the name of the Lord, even after his home and his heart had been emptied of their treasures. This could not have been an easy statement of faith to declare. But, as we read on, we find that Job also had a good deal of faith in himself, in his own goodness and faithfulness and uprightness. His friends were of little help. Badgering him about his own sin and guilt, essentially saying that, somehow, it was Job's sin that had brought this calamity upon him, they missed the point altogether. They kept trying to convince Job that he must have done *something* to deserve such suffering. All the time, Job defended his integrity and his good intentions. Neither he nor his friends had the eyes to see under the surface to what the real issues were.

Like a good mystery writer, the author takes us behind the scenes and lets us eavesdrop on a conversation that Job and his friends never hear. At the very beginning of the story he pulls aside the curtain and says to his readers: "In order to understand what happens to Job when he loses everything, you have to see what happened before that day. You have to see what was going on in heaven in order to see clearly what is going on in Job." And from that little peek, we know at least two things.

First, we know that Job is never, *never* forgotten by God. The dreadful events visited upon Job are tools of the devil himself, but, even so, God has set a limit upon the devil's harassment. Job is one of heaven's own sons, and God will not allow any power over Job's life to supersede his own. Every bit of Job's suffering, as was every bit of his prosperity, is in the hands of God. Second, we know that Job's sin did not cause his suffering, but neither did his faith deliver him from it. In the end (as we will see tomorrow) God saved Job and restored his good fortunes. Until that point, the story reveals a man who knew himself to be impoverished in every way but one—in himself. In other words, up to this point in his life, he had more faith in the strength of his own faith than he had in the strength of his God.

Both our risings and our fallings are intimately known to God, and he will have a purpose for both. The fact that we cannot see or understand that purpose has nothing to do with its ultimate accomplishment. Sometimes our faith is weak, barely breathing, but this in no way weakens the God in whom we place that faith. The richness of his love and power cannot be diminished by our poverty. "Blessed be the name of the Lord."

REFLECT | *Consider some of your own losses and sufferings. Looking back on them, what can you now see about the ways in which God was at work? How can this help you as you consider your present disappointments or pains?*

Day 4   Knowing God / Knowing Yourself

READ | Job 40:1–9; 42:1–17

I had heard of thee by the hearing of the ear, but now my eye sees thee;
therefore I despise myself and repent in dust and ashes. (vv. 5b–6)

God appears only twice in the story of Job, at the beginning, behind the scenes, and then again at the end, speaking directly to Job in the presence of his friends. In between, we imagine God listening in to the questioning and debating that is going on, waiting for just the right opportunity to inject himself into the conversation. That moment comes when all of Job's defenses come to an end, all his accusations against God cease, and all his arguments have been made. There is nothing more to say. Then, the silence is broken and Job is confronted by a new Voice coming out of the whirlwind: "Who is this that darkens counsel by words without knowledge? Gird up your loins like a man, I will question you, and you shall declare to me" (38:2–3). In other words: "I have been patiently listening to all your so-called wisdom, your allegations against me, your arguments and claims. Now, it is time for me to speak, and I have a few questions for you."

From time to time, God puts us in our place, not vindictively, not meanly, but always firmly. The questions he put to Job were all designed to remind his beloved child that God was God, and that Job was not. In the midst of his suffering, Job spent his breath defending his innocence and integrity against the counsel of his friends. In doing so, he was actually accusing God of being capricious and unjust. He was claiming that he had the proper view of things, that his own knowledge and righteousness were sufficient to see him through his troubles. As imperfect as they were, Job's friends were telling him to be quiet and listen, but they finally stopped speaking to him, says the writer, "because he was righteous in his own eyes" (32:1).

It was, so to speak, "his own eyes" that Job was having trouble with. His vision of God and of himself were both severely impaired, but he did not know it. So God set out to correct his eyesight. The sufferings of Job are almost unimaginable. But, as we discussed yesterday, they took place always under God's strong and wise supervision and were used by God for a good and loving purpose. Job could perceive none of this, in part because he was so busy telling everyone what he thought was going on.

I am not sure that Job ever really expected that God would listen to all his ranting, or that God would have something to say in response. I am not sure that we expect it either. But once God does enter the conversation—through the voice of his Spirit, of friends, of the circumstances themselves—everything changes. We come to realize that many things we thought we knew about God, we really did not know at all, and that we really knew even less about ourselves. As with the difference between seeing a blurry picture and meeting the real person, we, like Job, are dumbstruck by the difference. And that is what opens the way to new insights, to a renewed vision of God, and, really, to an entirely new life.

REFLECT | *What have you discovered about yourself in recent weeks, that has also revealed to you something more about God? How about the other way around? In what area of your life is God asking you to be still and to listen?*

Day 5   Failure: The Soil of Salvation

READ | Psalm 51

Create in me a clean heart, O God, and put a new and right spirit within me. (v. 10)

The heading for this psalm reads: "A Psalm of David, when Nathan the prophet came to him, after he had gone in to Bathsheba." This tells us immediately that these timeless words grew out of the most shameful episode in David's life (2 Samuel 11 and 12). His disobedience and lust led him to an adulterous liaison with Bathsheba, the wife of Uriah. When David found that she was carrying his child, he plotted to have Uriah killed in battle, to cover up his sin. Then David took Bathsheba for his own wife. Not a very pretty picture of the king who is called "a man after God's own heart."

But God was not finished with his servant. He sent the prophet Nathan to confront David with his deceit and cruelty. "You are the man!" must have been chilling words to David's ears. More important, they were heart-rending words to his soul. David repented and the 51st psalm was his prayer.

For generations, both this story and this psalm have been vivid reminders that God does not give up on his frail and wayward children. David remains a hero of the faith, as much because of his failings as because of his victories. He and all those other biblical figures, whose flaws have been recorded for all time to read, are presented to us as examples of God's faithfulness and deliverance *in the midst* of defeat, *despite* defeat, *because* of defeat. In fact, the entire Bible is an account of how God has been dealing with failure ever since time began. There is a medieval Christmas carol that actually gives thanks to God that Adam and Eve ate of the forbidden tree because, had they not, we would never have known the Savior. This is a poetic way of saying that God is so just and merciful, so powerful and so gracious, that he is able to bring forth the best from the ashes of the worst. If the worst had not happened, we may never have known God's best.

Failure, therefore, should never become the breeder of more failure, nor relapse the occasion for giving up. We must remember that our adversary's real intention through temptation is not to cause us to fall into sin, but to prevent us from getting back up to hope.

The momentary pleasure we derive from our indulgence is scarcely as destructive as the devastating sense of condemnation, guilt, and despair that follows. This is when David's prayer comes in handy. Humbled and chastened under the weight of our own failings, we go as quickly as we can to the throne of a holy and loving Savior, not to be excused but pardoned. "Once again, O God, I am in need of your saving grace," we pray.

David lived many more years following that fateful spring. They were years of more blessing and more trials, more victories and more failures. Through them all, David remained "a man after God's own heart." Under his reign the land of promise was secured, and from his house came forth the seed of salvation. What amazing things the Gardener can grow from such desolate soil!

REFLECT | *When have you let failure or relapse become the occasion for giving up? The prophet Jeremiah wrote that God's mercies "are new every morning" (Lamentations 3:23). For what "old" area in your life must you remember that promise and begin again, today?*

Day 6   A New Creation

READ | John 8:1–11

Neither do I condemn you; go, and do not sin again. (v. 11)

Speaking of "new mercies every morning"—here is
a story for the heavy-hearted soul. Try to imagine for a
moment what it must have been like for this poor woman
to be cornered by a mob of men and dragged into the
presence of Jesus. The sheer embarrassment must have
been excruciating, not to mention the fear that must have
gripped her by the throat. Death was only a few stone-throws
away. Since she had actually "been caught in adultery" (why
and how, one wonders), there was no question of her guilt—
nor of the required punishment. What is worse is that, in the
eyes of these sanctimonious scribes and Pharisees, she was
simply a means to an end. Her sin and shame meant nothing
to them. Neither did her life. She stood in the midst of them
as nothing more than an object lesson, a trap to be sprung
on this so-called prophet and rabbi.

Was the woman tempted to think that Jesus did not care
either, as he bent over and scribbled in the sand? Did he
even look at her before he turned his eyes to the ground?
And what was he writing? What could be more important
than the crisis at hand? The silence that followed must
have been the deepest and longest she had ever known.
What would he answer to their question? What would he
say about her?

We usually read this story as a lesson against self-
righteousness and judgmental attitudes toward others. As
the apostle Paul asked the Romans, "Who is in a position

to condemn?" Certainly none of these men. Certainly none of us. But all the time this showdown is taking place, this poor woman is standing there with only her sin and guilt for company. Eventually, under the weight of their own shame and unease, all these men turn away and leave her alone. Alone, that is, but for One other, who is stooping and writing in the dirt once again.

I wonder, sometimes, if the confusion she felt then, alone in Jesus' presence, was not even greater than what she felt when she was surrounded by her accusers. She knew clearly what they thought about her. I wonder if she was more worried about what he thought. They all turned away and left, but what if he did, too? All that mattered now was what he would do, or say . . . but he was still writing in the dust . . . and she was waiting.

I like to think that Jesus was mimicking his Father as he hunched over the earth that day.

In the Garden, his Father had first formed man of the dust of the earth, and certainly that meant that he had gotten his hands dirty. He had created something from nothing and then, out of grains of sand, he had sculpted his own image, and breathed into his likeness the breath of life. I like to think that with his finger working in the dust and with the word he was about to speak into the silence, Jesus was doing some creating of his own, some re-creating. And behold, it was very good.

"Therefore, if any one is in Christ, he is a new creation; the old has passed away, behold, the new has come." (2 Corinthians 5:17)

REFLECT | *Wait . . . listen. What is Jesus saying to you?*

Day 7   Do Not Lose Heart

READ | Luke 18:1–8

And he told them a parable to the effect that they ought always to pray and not lose heart. (v. 1)

We all know the frustration and discouragement that comes with unanswered prayer. "I'm praying, but I don't know if God is listening." "I've been praying about that for years, and nothing is any different." "I don't think there's much point in my praying about that any more." Have you ever noticed how the teachings of Jesus seem to anticipate our problems and confusions? Almost as if he answers a question before we even ask it? The story of the unjust judge and the importunate widow is just such a teaching.

Of course, Jesus is not telling us that God is like this callous, selfish judge (though he may be telling us that this is what we sometimes think of God). What he is doing, however, is presenting such an extreme example of heartlessness that making any comparison with God whatsoever is actually laughable. "If even this judge— who has such disdain for God and who doesn't care one whit about people—if even he will finally listen to a poor widow's persistent pleadings, how much more will God, who has nothing but compassion and justice in his heart, answer the cries of his children."

Jesus must have known how prone we are to discouragement when we do not see the answers to our prayers *when* we want to see them. He must have known our penchant for giving up and giving in. According to

John's Gospel, many of his disciples (there were more than the central "twelve") "drew back and no longer went along with him" when his message either struck too close to home or when its demands grew too difficult (John 6:66). There is little difference between that and turning away from God because we think he is no longer listening, no longer caring.

"Losing heart" is a common, though dangerous, occurrence in the Christian's life. The challenges we face can be debilitating, and the failures we suffer can be demoralizing. Jesus never takes them for granted, nor underestimates the potential they have for wearing down our resolve. What he asks of us, however, is that we neither stop nor wander away when we are in the midst of such circumstances, that we not give up on him when we are tempted to believe the hellish lie that he has given up on us; that we instead believe him when he tells us that God loves us and hears our prayers. "Keep asking," he is saying, for when your voice is lost to prayer, then your heart cannot be far behind.

REFLECT | *In what area of your life have you "lost heart," or given up? Where is God asking you to believe him more than you believe yourself? What prayer can you pray to help you do that?*

Week Ten Fear: Faith In The Wrong Person

Day 1   No Spirit of Fear

READ | 2 Timothy 1

For God did not give us a spirit of timidity, but a spirit of power and love and self-control. (v. 7)

Timothy was a young leader in the church and a colleague of the apostle Paul. It is clear from these letters, and from the other times that Paul mentions him in correspondence, that Timothy was a valued co-worker who, personally as well as professionally, meant a great deal to his mentor. The King James Version of the Bible translates verse 7 like this: "For God hath not given us the *spirit of fear*, but of power and love and of a sound mind." Paul was apparently writing to Timothy, in part, to encourage him to remain faithful to God's call in the face of trial and danger.

Fear takes many forms. On the one hand, fear is a useful reaction to have in sudden times of peril, and it can avert us from foolish risks or careless decisions. Fear can be an early and effective signal, warning us to flee from approaching harm and to seek protection. But, fear can also be a dark shadow that clouds our vision and prevents us from seeing things as they really are. When it becomes panic or depression, fear can become so debilitating that it actually prevents us from reacting, or acting. Then, "paralyzed with fear" can be an apt description for the soul as well as for the body. When fear whispers (or screams) that there is no place to run, then giving up appears as the only alternative.

When you stop to think about it, then, fear is really a form of unbelief. It acts as if, in any particular threatening situation, God is absent or unable to help. Fear does not recognize the irresistible power and the limitless love that God's presence brings in times of need. It sees only the danger. Put another way, fear is a form of belief, but in the wrong thing or person. We say that we trust God, and to a great extent we do. But, frightening situations usually reveal to us the things that we are really counting on, because they let us down. They show us the things we really believe to be the source of our strength, because those sources run dry. I am afraid because none of the things I depend upon are dependable enough to help and protect me—least of all, myself. I am afraid because I know I haven't the ability to be my own strength and protection. I feel helpless . . . and then I feel afraid.

But fear is not meant to have the last word. As a tool it is quite useful, but as a master it is inept and oppressive. As a tool it leads us to safety, but as a master it only turns us away from God. Remember the response of Adam when God came searching for him in the Garden: "I was afraid of thee . . . and I hid myself" (Genesis 3:10).

The truth is that we do not have to live in fear. Yes, fear lives in us all, but "God hath not given us the spirit of fear, but of power (his power), and of love (living in his love) and of a sound mind (seeing things for what they really are)." This week, we will discuss some of the fears that are most common to us all. Naming them gets us halfway toward overcoming them, because often fear is actually the hidden force that lies behind many of our more obviously misdirected words and actions. (Remember what we observed earlier about the best defense being a good offense?) We have also added a prayer at the conclusion of each of this week's reflections. If one of fear's deceptive tricks is to lead us away from God, then prayer is just the thing we need to send us in the opposite direction.

> O God, who has been a refuge and strength through all generations, be my refuge today in every time and circumstance of need. Be my guide through all that is dark and doubtful. Be my guard against all that threatens my spirit's welfare. Be my strength in time of testing. Gladden my heart with thy peace; through Jesus Christ my Lord. Amen.
> (John Baillie, 1886–1960,
> *Oxford Book of Prayer*, 123, adapt.)

REFLECT | *What are some of your present fears? How do you know when you are afraid? What are the signs?*

Day 2   Fear of Others

READ | John 20:19–31

The doors being shut where the disciples were, for fear of the Jews, Jesus came and stood among them and said to them, "Peace be with you." (v. 19)

If any group of people ever had legitimate cause to be afraid, the disciples were that group. Their Leader had been arrested, maligned, beaten, and, finally, crucified as an enemy of the state and the temple. The disciples were known associates of this criminal—they believed and preached the same message that he had taught, and they were commissioned by him to carry on with the cause. There was every reason for them to assume that, if discovered and seized, they would face from their captors the same treatment as their Lord. So, "for fear" of these men, they gathered secretly and hid behind closed doors.

The anxieties we suffer for fear of what others might do to us, or say about us, or think of us, may not include the fear of death, but they can still cause us to "shut the door of our hearts," lest our true selves be discovered. The prospect of being vulnerable and transparent with others can be very threatening, even when we know rationally that no one means us any harm. We have inherited from our forebears an innate fear of being known, especially with all our flaws and defects. "If he/she really knew . . . what I am like . . ," we fearfully wonder. Then we usually keep the door shut.

But neither the doors of the house nor the doors of our heart can shut out the Risen Jesus: neither can they shut us in from him. The latches were fixed, says the Gospel writer, and still Jesus came and stood among his beloved. The sight of his face and the sound of his voice must have driven away all their fears. "Peace be with you," he said, with his pierced hands outstretched and his wounded side displayed.

These fearful few went on to turn the world upside-down with their bravery and love. Of the Twelve, only John died an old man of natural causes. All the rest met and welcomed a martyr's death, bright reflections of their Lord's own unquenchable flame. From such inauspicious beginnings—a tiny huddle of frightened souls trembling behind closed doors—Jesus brought forth his church, and all of hell itself cannot prevail against it.

"Peace be with you," Jesus says to you and me. He gently comes and passes effortlessly through all the barriers we set up as he makes his way into the midst of our hearts. And he brings others with him—friends and family, sisters and brothers in Christ, people known and unknown, kind and unkind. Unlike our Lord, however, they have to use the door, and it is left to us to either open it or to leave it shut. If we lift the latches and give them a chance to come in, we will find that any fears we have of them are quickly dispelled by Jesus' presence. But this takes some time and practice. Opening our hearts to others—letting them see the blemishes on our souls, the weaknesses in our character, even the fears that compel us to keep them out in the first place—this is done with one little decision at a time. In the end, we will find that nothing they can ever do, or say, or think can really harm us. Like the apostles, we may find that the peace of Jesus is more than enough protection.

> Christ with me, Christ before me, Christ behind me,
> Christ within me, Christ beneath me, Christ above me,
> Christ on my right, Christ on my left. . . .
> Christ in the heart of everyone who thinks of me,
> Christ in the mouth of everyone who speaks to me,
> Christ in every eye that sees me,
> Christ in every ear that hears me.
> —*Canticle of St. Patrick*
> (Phyllis Tickle, *The Divine Hours: Prayers for Summertime,* 312)

REFLECT | *What are you most afraid of someone else doing to you, or saying about you, or thinking of you? What are some of the fearful barriers you use to shut out other people? What one person can you let further in today? How?*

Day 3   Fear of Conflict

READ │   Psalm 27

Though a host encamp against me, my heart shall not fear. (v. 3)

Often our fear of others has to do with our fear of conflict. In other words, it is not so much the other person we fear, as it is the hurt and other disturbing sensations we experience when we are at odds with one another. Quarrels and discord arouse some of the emotions and attitudes within us that we most want to keep still—anger, self-righteousness, helplessness, uncertainty, and even hatred. In the face of conflict we fear that we are likely to be harmed, perhaps as much by what arises from within us as by what comes at us from outside us. In any case, we fear conflict and the potential it brings for injuring us. As we have seen, however, conflict has always been a fellow-traveler on the road of discipleship, and there is no real way to avoid his company, no matter how much we may try to steer clear of him.

David, as we know, was a soldier as well as a king. In fact, it was because he knew so much warfare and bloodshed that God prohibited him from building the Temple in Jerusalem (1 Chronicles 22:8). What David did build, however, was a kingdom, dedicated to the worship of God and to the fulfillment of his purposes. In that endeavor, and despite his flaws, David never wavered. So when we read the 27th psalm, we are reading the words of a man who was willing to face conflict, even risk his own destruction, for the sake of something greater and more lasting than himself. In order to do the will of God, David was willing to accept conflict as a part of his life, so long as he knew that God would be his salvation.

A word of caution is in order here—this has nothing to do with the presumptuous notion that "God is on *my* side and therefore *I* will prevail." Some of us think of a fight (or even spoil for a fight) as an opportunity to win and, by winning, to feel even stronger about ourselves. The source of David's confidence was not his own rightness but rather the loving protection of God. His interest was in doing God's will, and the only way that could be accomplished was by God's strength, not his own. He sings his song of assurance in praise of God's protection and deliverance: "He will hide me in his shelter in the day of trouble; he will conceal me under the cover of his tent, he will set me high upon a rock" (v. 5). There is nothing whatsoever in these words in praise of David's own might or valor. His ability to face conflict is firmly rooted in the Lord, who is "the stronghold" of his life.

When our paths cross with the unwelcome company of conflict, to whose strength do we turn for our defense? When those situations arise that threaten our security, our peace of mind, or the lives and welfare of those we love, do we "wait for the Lord," or do we muster up our own might and count on our own abilities to win the battle? If we do the latter, then we are consigned to the fears that accompany such misplaced trust. In contrast to trusting in the "mighty fortress" of God, Martin Luther wrote: "Did we in our own strength confide, our striving would be losing." If we do the former, however, if we cry aloud to the Lord and seek his face, then we can take courage in the face of conflict, and we can know the joyful melody of David's song.

Almighty God, who sees that we have no power of
ourselves to help ourselves: Keep us, both outwardly in
our bodies and inwardly in our souls, that we may be
defended from all adversities which may happen to the
body and from all evil thoughts which may assault and
hurt the soul; through Jesus Christ our Lord. Amen.

—*Gregorian Sacramentary*

(John Wallace Suter Jr., ed., *The Book of English Collects*, 77)

REFLECT | *What situations are you facing right now that
are beyond your own strength? With whom are you most afraid to be
in conflict? Why?*

Day 4   Fear of Death

READ | Hebrews 2

*Since therefore the children share in flesh and blood, he himself
likewise partook of the same nature, that through death he might
destroy him who has the power of death, that is, the devil, and deliver
all those who through fear of death were subject to lifelong bondage.
(vv. 14–15)*

John Wesley was brought up in a strict, devout home.
His father was a clergyman of the Church of England, and
his mother, Susanna, was also the child of a clergyman.
The entire family, for generations, had been trained in the
Bible and in the spiritual life. John writes, however, that
he was ceaselessly plagued by one anxious thought—the
fear of dying. Other fears he was able to conquer, but not
this one, at least not until the night he found his heart

"strangely warmed" at the thought that God's love and his Son's redemptive death on the cross was for him, for John. Following that hour, when he knew Christ to be his only Lord and his only Savior, Wesley noticed one thing in particular—he no longer feared death. And when the fear of death came knocking upon his door, he forbade its entry by hurling in its face his trust in the Risen Christ.

According to the writer of Hebrews, the fear of death is the subjugator of all humanity. We all live under its foreboding shadow. For some, the very idea of dying—of being no more, cut off from loved ones and from the joys of life, to face an unknown eternity—can be terrifying. No wonder the world, by exalting youthfulness and mastering sickness, spends so much time and energy creating the illusion that we can live forever. The alternative is simply too fearful for us.

Christians have never been taught to treat death lightly, or to pretend that it is anything other than the mortal enemy of life. It is clear from Scripture that death had no place in God's good creation until it entered the world through sin. This puts death and the devil in league with one another, and many of us have experienced the darkness it brings— when it steals from us someone we love, or breaks into our lives with no warning, leaving no time to prepare. At such disruptively devastating times, all romantic notions of death being "just another step on the journey" quickly take a back seat to the utter sense of helplessness and to the raw anger and fear that takes hold of us.

Reconciling ourselves to death's inevitability with more than weak resignation or quiet bitterness requires that our hearts be reconciled with the Lord of both life and death.

He died in order to conquer death, and his rising again is the evidence of his success. Facing death, our own or someone else's, with courage and humility, requires that, in the midst of our honest grief and struggle to understand, we also trust and believe.

Someone has said that the best way to prepare to die is to die daily—for the sake of Christ to take up our own crosses and to follow him. In his great chapter of exultation in the Resurrection of Christ, the apostle Paul says of his own life, "I die every day!" (1 Corinthians 15:31). For Jesus, the cross was no surprise; it was the completion of an entire life lived, not to do his own will, but the will of his Father who sent him (John 6:38). Perhaps this is the secret to defeating our fear of death—by giving up our lives more and more along the way. Then, by the time we arrive at death's door, it will hold no surprises for us and we need not be afraid of it. It really will be "just another step along the journey."

Save us while waking, Lord, and guard us while sleeping, that when we awake we may watch with Christ, and when we sleep we may rest in peace. Amen.

(An antiphon for night prayer)

REFLECT | *Describe what your own fear of death feels like. What was your most recent experience of death? How did you face it?*

Day 5   Fear of Want

R E A D | Matthew 6:19–34

Therefore I tell you, do not be anxious about your life, what you shall eat, or what you shall drink, nor about your body, what you shall put on. . . . Do not be anxious about tomorrow, for tomorrow will be anxious for itself. (vv. 26 and 34a)

What one of us does not know the anxiety of worrying about the future? Especially prone to these fears are those who bear primary responsibility for the care of others, for children or parents or spouse. "What will we do?" "How will we make it?" "What if we don't have enough?" "Who will take care of me?" You can add your own particular anxious question.

Jesus teaches that the lasting answer to our anxiety will never be found by scurrying about, restlessly searching for everything we think we need, and then hoarding it up in some stockpile. This, he warns, will give us only a false sense of security, for such stockpiles are deceivingly small when compared to enormous need, and regularly susceptible to decay and ruin. Jesus does not advocate our being foolishly naïve about the future, either, as if life held no risks and we would face no failures. He talks about the dangers of fear and anxiety precisely because he knows the fleeting and perishable nature of this life, and he knows that we have not yet learned how to live it with peace and confidence. From whence is such peace and confidence to come—that is the question he is answering.

First, Jesus says, take a lesson from the things that you see around you. Consider the created world itself. The apostle

Paul said that God's invisible nature can be perceived in the things that he has made, that what can be known about God and his ways is made plain by creation (Romans 1:19–20). I sometimes envy those who live closer to the earth than I. I know that I miss much of the wisdom it has to offer. But I can still hear it in the words of Jesus. "Consider the lilies." "Look at the birds." "Touch the grass." If, as the Creator, God can clothe and feed and provide for all that *they* need, how very much more, as your Father, can and will he supply the things *you* require. God is neither blind to our need nor miserly in his giving. Jesus is telling his listeners that if they would be more trusting in God they would be less anxious for themselves. One or the other—fear or belief—will take up the majority of space in the human heart, and the choice will be ours.

Speaking of the human heart, however, Jesus gives a second instruction for overcoming anxiety: make it your first aim, above everything else you seek, to seek the kingdom of God. The reason we suffer so much anxiety about our futures is that the priorities of our hearts are upside-down. They are listed in the wrong order. It is a natural phenomenon of living that when we are faced with a demanding and seemingly insurmountable task, other less important tasks get set aside, even forgotten for a time. They become of less importance until the primary obligation confronting us has been accomplished. Our anxieties about the things of earth will diminish the more we focus on the things of heaven. Jesus says that there simply isn't enough room in our hearts for both.

A PRAYER

O God, facing all that is before us, we know not whether
we will live or die, but this we know: that all things are
ordered and sure in heaven. Everything is planned with
unerring wisdom and unbounded love by you, our God,
for you are love. Grant us in all things to see your hand;
through Jesus Christ our Lord. Amen.

(Rev. C. Simeon, 1759, adapt.)

REFLECT | *What are the things that make you most anxious
about the future? For what one particular anxiety will you trust God
today?*

Day 6   Fear of Humiliation

READ | Exodus 4:1–17

*But Moses said to the Lord, "Oh, my Lord, I am not eloquent, either
heretofore or since thou hast spoken to thy servant; but I am slow of
speech and of tongue." (v. 10)*

Today we approach a subject that can be somewhat
sensitive. But bear with me for a moment and see if this
does not make sense. Moses resisted God's call upon his life
because he was afraid. Biblical scholars tell us that Moses'
reference to being "slow of speech and of tongue" may have
had to do either with his fear of speaking in public (a *very*
common anxiety!), or to some kind of impediment in his
speech. In either case, Moses was clearly self-conscious about
this weakness and wanted nothing to do with an assignment
that required him to do the very thing that he was worst

at doing. During his argument with God, for a brief time, it seems that Moses feared being humiliated in the eyes of men more than he feared God. God was even willing to make a compromise in order to secure Moses' agreement. (We can all be grateful that God is not as quick as we are to move on when he meets resistance.)

In and of itself, humiliation is not something any of us seek. It can even be devastating. How many of us suffer wounds inflicted by the demeaning actions of others or by degrading events out of our own control? It is because of experiences like these, experiences that strike at our very dignity and sense of security, that Jesus came to heal us and make us whole. But the humiliations we receive at the hand of a loving God are designed to strike at something else, something deadly, something that separates us from God and from others. It is not our dignity as children of heaven that God is after—it is our pride as children of earth.

Humbling ourselves of our own free choice is an extremely difficult thing to do—and it's impossible to do without mixed motives. The very act of "trying to be humble" before others betrays a lack of genuine humility, because humility, by its very definition, is entirely un*self*conscious! This is why we need what comes from outside us to humble us, to humiliate us. In the hands of God, humiliations come through those closest to us and through strangers, through the contradictions and failures of life, even through the ways in which God calls us to serve him. Through each of these occasions, God is working to bring down a child of Adam and Eve in order to raise up a child of God. We can be certain that God will be the defender of our dignities and reputations, for love's design is to heal what is broken and to mend what is wounded. But we can be equally sure that he will do everything in love's power to make low those "mountains and hills" that stand against what is best for his own daughters and sons (Luke 3:5). And pride is the highest mountain of all.

The early church teacher Cyril of Alexandria wrote of Jesus: "He became like us that we might become like him. The work of the Spirit seeks to transform us by grace into a perfect copy of his humbling." It would appear, therefore, that the call of Moses was as much for his benefit as it was for the benefit of Israel's children. God was making a man even as he was making a nation. It required only that, despite his fear of humiliation, Moses say "yes."

A PRAYER

Lord Jesus, you humbled yourself to become like one of us, and to be born into the world for our salvation. Teach me the grace of humility; root out of my heart all pride and haughtiness, and so fashion me after your holy likeness in this world, that in the world to come I may reflect your everlasting glory; for your mercy's sake. Amen.

(Bishop Walsham How, d. 1823, adapt.)

REFLECT | *What are some of the humiliating experiences that you have suffered that make you fear humiliation today? In what area(s) have you already found that a humiliation actually worked to your benefit? What is God asking of you right now, that you are resisting because you are afraid of humiliation?*

Day 7   When I am Afraid

READ │   Psalm 56
When I am afraid, I put my trust in thee. (v. 3)

During this week we have visited with some our most basic fears—fear of others, fear of conflict, fear of death, fear of want, and fear of humiliation. Today, we turn once more to the psalms for a final word of encouragement.

It is clear from this prayer that the writer is in great danger. His enemies are very real and very strong. He is outnumbered and overpowered. But it is equally clear that there are some very real alternatives to the psalmist's fear. A few simple words tell us what they are:

When I am afraid, I put my trust in thee (v. 3)—A small child is sometimes afraid in the dark. A noise wakes her up and her bleary eyes see shapes moving on the wall like menacing figures. She pulls the covers up over her head in the hopes that the shadows will go away, but this doesn't stop her imagination from "seeing" even worse things. Fear has now taken on a life of its own, and soon turns to panic. In a fraction of a second, she makes her decision. Risking everything (especially being grabbed by the monster that is now under the bed), she throws off the covers, makes a single daring leap to the door, runs down the hallway like the wind, and bounds into her parents' bed. There, in the comfort of their embrace, and with only a soothing "shhh" from their lips, she ever so slowly falls back to a peaceful sleep.

When you are afraid, child, where do you run?

This I know, that God is for me (v. 9)—Confidence is rarely innate to our characters. More likely, it is born of repeated positive experiences that tell us that our trust is being put in the right place. In other words, confidence really is "built." The dancer who must fling herself into the arms of her partner may at first hold back. She tries to relax, but she stiffens each time her feet leave the floor, and her own arms brace for the expected fall. But the fall never comes. Each time, her partner's arms are there to receive her. Not once does he falter, despite how awkwardly and hesitantly she comes. With every successful jump she finds her trust in him growing until, finally, she throws herself without caution, and the dance becomes all grace.

What can you do now, child, with what you already know about me?

What can man do to me? (v. 11)—Plenty, I might answer. With the psalmist I might describe all that trampling and lurking they do, thinking bad things about me and working to frustrate my every move. But really, can man do something to destroy me? Can he separate me from the love of God? Can she take away my birthright as a child of God? Can they stop God's work in my life? Can they keep me from putting my trust in the God who is for me?

Do you know, child, that the answer to all these questions is "no"?

God's might to uphold me,

God's wisdom to guide me,

God's eye to look before me,

God's ear to hear me,

God's word to speak to me,

God's hand to guard me,

God's way to lie before me,

God's shield to protect me,

God's hosts to save me.

—St. Patrick

(Phyllis Tickle, *The Divine Hours:
Prayers for Autumn and Wintertime*, 312)

REFLECT | *Consider the questions that are asked in this reflection. How would you answer them?*

Week Eleven Who Has The Reins Anyway?

Day 1　According to Your Will

READ | Luke 1:26-38

And Mary said, "Behold, I am the handmaid of the Lord; let it be to me according to your word." (v. 38)

Ten weeks ago, we began this series of reflections by looking at the terrible consequences of Adam and Eve's disobedience to God—the severing of their relationship with their Creator and with one another. It was as if a beautiful vessel formed by God, with the intention that it always be brimming with his life and love, was violently shattered on the rocks into countless fragments and splinters. Only God, out of sheer mercy and grace, could see the possibility of putting it all back together, and he set forth to do just that. You and I are now part of this miraculous re-creative plan. Every blessing we receive and every trial we undergo, every circumstance we encounter and every person in our lives—all these and much more, God uses in order to gather and mend and reshape the broken pieces of his own sacred handiwork. All he asks of us is that, unlike our first parents, we agree this time with the way he intends to do things, that we not try to come up with our own better ideas, but, instead, trust that he knows what he is doing.

For all this re-creation to even be possible, of course, God sent forth a "new Adam" to open the way for us (1 Corinthians 15:45). With the coming of Jesus Christ, God started over, not by throwing everything away but by reclaiming it all for a new and even better purpose. But in order to do so, he counted on one of us to agree with his plan. A young Hebrew girl was his choice: Mary, who became the mother of our Lord and, in a sense, a "new Eve." She was very much favored and "full of grace," not only because of the unimaginable honor (and burden) she would know for bringing Jesus into the world, but also because she was able so freely and wholly to give herself to God's will. Mary's "let it be to me according to your word" was the response that God had been looking for in the Garden. Adam and Eve (with a little help) rejected God's plans in favor of their own. In every way they are the prime examples of what happens in the kingdom of God when someone other than the King is in charge. Mary, on the other hand, is the prime example of what happens when God has his way, when his will prevails, and when we agree to his purposes.

A "disciple" is literally a "student." This means that, by following Jesus, you and I are learning things that we did not know before. One of the most important lessons we must learn, one that is taught at absolutely every "grade level" of the Christian life, is that God is in charge and that his ways, not ours, are always and everywhere the best. And the reason the lesson is taught so often is that we don't learn it the first time, or the second, or the third. Not surprisingly, given what happened in the Garden, this is one of the hardest subjects to master.

"Who is in charge of my life?" "Whose way of doing things is the best?" "Whose hands are really holding the reins?" These are the questions we are looking at this week. Of course, we all know what the *right* answer is, but, unlike Mary, when the question is asked at very specific moments we are often very, very slow to raise our hands and answer with our own voices. Why is that? This week, by reflecting on some of the choices made by a few other "students" who have already passed through this classroom, we may be able to better understand what we are up against.

REFLECT | *In what kinds of circumstances do you find it most difficult to want God's will? Why? What does it mean to you for God to "be in charge" of your life? What does it not mean?*

Day 2 Wrestling With God

READ | Genesis 32

And Jacob was left alone; and a man wrestled with him until the breaking of the day. (v. 24)

The story of Jacob's nocturnal wrestling match with the angel of the Lord illustrates for us the lengths to which God is willing to go in order to convince us that his ways are true and good. It is a good image for our own scuffles with the Almighty.

We have had some insight into Jacob's life already, when we discussed the preferential treatment he received from his mother and that he, in turn, passed on to his son. In neither case, you remember, did their "idolatry"—putting their desires for their children before the righteousness of God—produce good results (Week 4). But there is much more to his story. The writer of Genesis presents Jacob as an ambitious conniver, even in birth, when he came forth from his mother's womb grasping the heel of his twin, Esau. From that very day, Jacob lived up to the meaning of his name, "he who supplants." By his shrewd scheming he successfully stole his brother's birthright, deceived his father into imparting to him the paternal blessing meant for Esau, and made a fortune for himself off his future father-in-law, Laban. What is more, by the time he left Laban's employment he had become the father of eleven sons who, together with his youngest son, Joseph, would be the patriarchs of the twelve tribes of Israel. Jacob had "climbed the ladder," rung by rung, and made of himself a great man.

However, there was still this matter of swindling his brother that had gone unsettled for years. Hearing the news that Esau and his men were approaching his camp, Jacob came up with one more plan for getting what he wanted, this time his brother's pardon. (It turns out, of course, that Esau was happy and held no grudge whatsoever.) These are the circumstances in which we find Jacob at the river Jabbok, nervously waiting for what the coming dawn will bring. There is nothing more he can do. And this is precisely when God chooses to meet him, face-to-face and hand-to-hand. Through those few dark hours, it is as if Jacob's entire life of self-will and self-sufficiency is being played out with God on that muddy shore. (Another act of "re-creation" by the hand of God?)

The remarkable thing is that God would come down to his creature in such a way, and actually engage with him so intimately and tirelessly. It almost seems as if he has been waiting for just the right time and place to have this struggle with Jacob. God is not averse to having us take hold of him and "wrestle." He looks for our doubts and questions and even our accusations against him to be forthright and honest. He may even be waiting for us to "have it out" with him, knowing that this may be the only way for us to know the strong grip of his love and his truth.

Who is the declared winner in this contest? Is it Jacob, who "strove with God and with men, and prevailed" (v. 28), or is it God, who brought an abrupt end to the fight by dislocating Jacob's hip with only a touch of his finger? In fact, don't they both win? God wins by demonstrating to Jacob, through affliction, that he is merely mortal and no match for the almighty arm of God. God has won his chosen son over to a new relationship of trust and dependence. Jacob wins, too . . . and for the exact same reason.

REFLECT | *Think about your own wrestling with God. What are you after—your own way or God's blessing? Over what issue in your life right now do you need to take hold of God and not let go until you receive his blessing?*

Day 3   Faithless Planning

READ | Genesis 15:1–6; 16:1–16

And he believed the Lord; and he reckoned it to him as righteousness. (15:6)

Jacob's grandfather was Abraham, and, as they say, the apple doesn't fall far from the tree. We first met Abraham ("Abram" at that time) when God called him to take his wife Sarai and to leave his country and his family and go to a new land which God would show him (see Genesis 12:1ff). From this unexceptional couple God intended to raise up a great nation through whom he would bless the whole earth.

As usual, there was a significant and all-too evident problem with this plan—Abraham and Sarai had no children, and no prospects whatsoever for ever having children.

The writer of Genesis tells us that God repeated his promise to Abraham a number of times, and each time it was greeted with acceptance and faith. In fact, Abraham has become a lasting example of what it means to believe God and trust in his promises. Writing to the Christians in Rome, the apostle Paul commended Abraham for his faith and exhorted his readers to imitate him: "No distrust made [Abraham] waver concerning the promise of God, but he grew strong in his faith as he gave glory to God, fully convinced that God was able to do what he had promised" (4:20–21). But wait. "*No* distrust"? What about this little incident with Hagar?

As we have observed before, the Bible (thankfully) makes no apologies for presenting its character's weaknesses as well as strengths. In the case of Abraham, the "father" of our faith, it is a temporary lapse of faith that, in some ways, endears him to us. It is not that Abraham doubted God's promise to make him the father of a people more numerous than the stars. It is just that, as time wore on and the promise was delayed, Abraham, with Sarai's encouragement, took upon himself the means for fulfilling that promise. In other words, he took things into his own hands.

Waiting upon God is one of the most difficult, yet important things that you and I can do in the Christian life. It is difficult because we are not patient people, and waiting on *anyone* tries what little patience we do have. In Abraham's case, God had a very specific plan, a very specific way he intended to carry out that plan, and a very specific schedule to be followed. In every way, God was in charge. But, after a long delay (is there such a thing on God's timetable?), and there was still no fulfillment in sight, Abraham and Sarai succumbed to the kind of temptation we can all understand—to do it themselves.

Sometimes, the struggle we have letting God have his way in our lives has less to do with our faith in his love than it has to do with our impatience with how that love is expressed. Our conviction that God's ways are best can be put severely to the test when we are waiting to see specific signs of those ways—a child's healing, a new job, reconciliation with a loved one, the answer to a prayer. These are among the many, many very concrete "waiting times" when our faith in God and our agreement with his plans are put to the test. Like Sarai and Abraham, we fail that test from time to time. In our impatience we either take things into our own hands and try to force an answer, or we simply give up altogether. But neither of those two alternatives brings about the will of God for our lives. The promise to Abraham and Sarai was fulfilled. Even their presumptive actions did not prevent it. What was required of them, and of us, was to believe . . . and to wait.

REFLECT | *What examples can you draw from your own life when waiting for God brought the better answer to your need? What are you waiting for these days? Where have you given up hope for any answer to come?*

Day 4　Do You Know What You Are Asking?

READ | Matthew 20:17–34

You know not what you are asking. Are you able to drink the cup I am to drink? (v. 22)

Mrs. Zebedee's prayers were not much different from our own, and her ambitious hopes for her sons are something we can all understand. She wanted the best for them, and, like most parents, she assumed that the "best" also meant the most prominent and important. Most of us would probably not be as brazenly obvious as she was when she approached Jesus, and we are left to wonder if the youthful James and John at first reddened with embarrassment when they heard her make her request. However, the fact that Jesus answered and addressed his questions to them seems to indicate that they had been part of the scheme all the time. In any event, here is a mother putting into words what most of us only think with our minds: I want my children to be successes. Of course, Mrs. Zebedee's forthrightness is what lends this story its degree of humor—but also its sense of tragedy. The things we can do to our children! Had she any idea then of the things her two sons would do and would suffer in the years to come, she would never have been so foolish.

This week we are reflecting on our need to let God have charge of our lives. Surely one of the most complex and difficult ways we do that is to let him have charge of those whom we love most. "Backing off" and letting God be God in the lives of our closest family and friends can be downright painful at times, especially when we see them in pain. Our own upbringings have instilled within us a whole list of do's and don'ts, of "I will always" and "I will nevers" that we apply to our own parenting. Some are helpful and some are not. But, with the realization that God loves our children, our families, and our friends far more than we do, also comes the realization that all the good intentions we can muster can only go so far. In the end, we have been entrusted only as stewards and never as owners of these souls. The only one entitled to that is God, their Creator and Redeemer.

With regard to our children, the world sometimes uses the idea that we have to "let them grow up." This is true, but I am inclined to think that the people who also need to "grow up"—that is, to become the men and women of faith that our children need—are we parents. I once read a sermon by a Russian Orthodox priest who said, "God gave children in order to raise their parents." More than anything else, our children need to know that God loves them and that his ways in their lives will always be the best ways. Then, above all else, they can want to love God and to know the joy of doing his will. This will always require that our faith grow up along with theirs, and that we grow older and stronger in our love for God and in our ability to trust him with everything that is important to us.

Years ago, a little prayer came to mind that I have prayed for my family ever since. Your own probably goes something like it. "Lord, _____ belongs to you. Have your way in her/his life, and may you come to mean more to her/him than anyone or anything else in the world. Amen." Mrs. Zebedee was right to pray for her children, for that is exactly what she was doing when she came to Jesus. In her own way, misdirected as it was, she wanted her sons to be close to Jesus, to always be in his company and to sit with him when he became king. But she didn't really know what she was asking. What parent does? This is why we need to let God be in charge.

REFLECT | *What is it that you most want for your children, for your family, for your closest friends? What does it mean for you to entrust them into God's hands? What will this require of you?*

Day 5   What Are You Doing, Lord?

READ | John 11:1–44
Martha said to Jesus, "Lord, if you had been here, my brother would not have died." (v. 21)

Martha, as we know already, was not shy about speaking her mind to Jesus. What is more, on the two occasions we know of from the Gospels, she is recorded with criticism in her voice: "Lord, do you really know what you are doing?"

On the first occasion, you remember, she was indignant that her sister Mary was sitting at Jesus' feet while leaving her to all the work in the kitchen. "Lord, do you not care?" she asked accusingly (Luke 10:40). Then, she essentially ordered Jesus to set her sister straight. This second occasion, recorded by John, is by far more serious. But still, Martha does not hesitate to question Jesus. As soon as she hears that he has entered the village she takes matters in hand and runs to meet him. The same criticizing question is in her tone—"Lord, what were you thinking?"—when she says, "If you had been here, this would not have happened." In the first instance, Martha is clearly put out. In the second, she is clearly in pain.

"Lord, do you really know what you are doing?" The question lies behind many of our conversations with God, especially in connection with the most painful and difficult circumstances in our lives. Illnesses, accidents, family problems, financial issues—these and many of life's disappointments and failures compel us again and again to ask, "Why, Lord?" This is an honest enough question, but it usually carries with it the conceited notion that, were we in charge, we never would have let the thing happen in the first place.

Martha's questioning continues even after Jesus begins to show signs of doing something. When he commands that Lazarus' tomb be opened, it is Martha who corrects him saying, "Are you kidding, Lord? Do you know what it is going to smell like?" Still the one to think that her view of things is the best, Martha is quick to call Jesus' view into question. "Lord, do you really know what you are doing?"

Jesus was patient with Martha as she stood before him back at the supper, essentially complaining that her sister was being lazy and that he was being indulgent in allowing it. But, on this occasion, at the death of her beloved brother, Martha needed more than patience—she needed comfort and assurance. Jesus read through her accusative tone and heard the cry of pain in her heart . . . and he answered it.

Is this not the image of grace itself? The Lord of all life submits himself to the controlling ways and questions of this woman, and gradually, gently brings her to look at things the way he sees them. What if Jesus *had* been in Bethany while Lazarus was sick? What if he had come *then* and healed Lazarus of his illness? Or, what if Martha had gotten her way and they *had not* taken away the stone? The raising of Lazarus turned out to be the radiant precursor of Jesus' own Resurrection. I will bet you that after that, Martha believed that Jesus really did know what he was doing!

REFLECT | *What are the circumstances in your life in which you are asking, "Lord, do you really know what you are doing"? How can you change that question into a genuine prayer for help?*

Day 6   Not This Way, Lord

READ | Matthew 16:13–28
But he turned and said to Peter, "Get behind me, Satan! You are a hindrance to me, for you are not on the side of God, but of men." (v. 23)

Wow! Now here is a confrontation that we would not want to be on the wrong side of! No discussion of people in the Bible who "wrestled" with God would be complete without a look at Peter.

Certainly we cannot fault Peter for his wanting Jesus to be kept safe from harm. It seems only natural. It *is* only natural. Peter loved Jesus. He wanted to see Jesus' work succeed. He wanted more and more people to find the same truth, the same help, the same hope that he and his fellow disciples had found listening to Jesus and following him. He believed that Jesus had a great future, and he was ready to do everything he could to insure that nothing should stand in the way.

But then Jesus introduces all this talk about betrayal and suffering and death in Jerusalem. Just a short time before he had confirmed Peter's God-given insight into Jesus' true identity—he was the Son of God, the Savior. Now he is talking about dying, and Peter will have none of it. Can you imagine his shock and pain when Jesus turned to him with that stinging rebuke: "Get behind me, Satan! You are a hindrance to me, for you are not on the side of God, but of men"? Maybe Peter took it in his stride. The Gospel writer discreetly omits any mention of his reaction. What he does record are Jesus' following words, in which he calls all of his followers to the same way of the cross that he himself walked. In many ways, it is at the same time both the least pleasant and the most promising aspect of discipleship that there is. But it is not a way that we would choose of our own accord.

Is it possible that, with the noblest of motives and even the strongest of affections, we can still find ourselves in opposition to the ways of God in our own lives or in the lives of others? Can we ever presume, given how mysterious and infinite are the divine designs, that we could fully grasp the most paradoxical of all—that life comes out of death, and that, therefore, death, in all the shapes it takes, may sometimes be the very best thing? "There is a way that seems right to a man," says the writer of Proverbs, "but its end is the way to death" (14:12). In a sense, this is exactly what Jesus was saying to Peter—that the way that seemed "right" to him, the way of self-preservation and security that he wanted to follow, was actually more a reflection of hell than of heaven. Had Peter's will prevailed over his Lord's, death would be the only way that any of us would know.

Peter the Apostle did us all a great favor that day when he so impulsively countered the words of our Lord. He helped us all to see where we might be doing the same thing ourselves.

"For my thoughts are not your thoughts, neither are your ways my ways, says the Lord. For as the heavens are higher than the earth, so are my ways higher than your ways and my thoughts than your thoughts." (Isaiah 55:8–9)

REFLECT | *Describe an event in which you were sure that you knew best, only to find that God had something even better in mind. Where can you see that your desire to protect others from pain may actually deny them of something even better?*

Day 7   Here Am I! Send Me

READ | Isaiah 6
In the year that King Uzziah died I saw the Lord sitting upon a throne, high and lifted up; and his train filled the temple. (v. 1)

We have spent a few days reflecting on the question of "who is in charge" of our lives. By their own "wrestlings" with God, a number of figures from the Bible have challenged us to consider where our own struggles may lie when it comes to giving over the reins to God. We cannot leave this topic without looking at one more figure who, like Mary, gave over those reins in a quick and humble fashion.

Isaiah, like all the prophets, was charged by God to proclaim a message to his people. Most often, that message was one of correction and warning—correction against the sins and wickedness of the people, and warnings of impending judgment if they did not change their ways. In Isaiah's case, however, that message also contains some of the most hopeful promises and the most beautiful language in all of the Old Testament.

—Behold, a young woman shall conceive, and bear a son, and shall call his name Immanuel. (7:14)

—For to us a child is born, to us a son is given. (9:6)

—The wolf shall dwell with the lamb, and the leopard shall lie down with the kid, and the calf and the lion and the fatling together, and a little child shall lead them. (11:6)

—And the ransomed of the Lord shall return, and come to Zion with singing; everlasting joy shall be upon their heads; they shall obtain joy and gladness, and sorrow and sighing shall flee away. (35:10)

—Comfort, comfort my people, says your God. Speak tenderly to Jerusalem, and cry to her, that her warfare is ended, that her iniquity is pardoned. (40:1)

—All we like sheep have gone astray; we have turned every one to his own way; and the Lord has laid on him the iniquity of us all. (53:6)

—The Spirit of the Lord is upon me, because the Lord has anointed me to bring good tidings to the afflicted; he has sent me to bind up the brokenhearted, to proclaim liberty to the captives, and the opening of the prison to those who are bound. (61:1)

All these quotations are by way of saying that Isaiah's "here am I" paved the way for God to reveal the heart of his plan for the salvation of the world. Isaiah, who for a few moments was mesmerized by a vision of the Lord in all his glory, said "yes" to a task that he did not yet comprehend. He could never have understood at that moment the purposes for which he was being called. He could never have imagined the golden tongue with which he would speak, nor the amount of light he would be shedding in a darkened world. He could never have dreamt then of the joy his message would inspire for centuries, nor the hope to which it would give birth.

What must Isaiah have seen that compelled him to such a swift and willing acceptance? Not "what," but "who," and so the question answers itself. For if we can see Jesus, if we can see him filling the temple of our hearts and hear his call echoing to us through all its chambers, if our love for him could be as pure as Mary's and our vision of him as clear as Isaiah's, then would we ever want any other to reign over our lives?

REFLECT | *What would it mean for you to say "yes" to God today? In what way is he asking you to say, "here am I"? What is he asking you to do?*

Week Twelve Come, Follow Me

Day 1   Blessings and Obstacles

READ | Numbers 13:1–14:10

If the Lord delights in us, he will bring us into this land and give it to us, a land which flows with milk and honey. (14:9)

Over the last few weeks, we have spent a good deal of time discussing some of the various obstacles that hinder us on our path of discipleship—things like jealousy and idolatry, anger and self-pity, vindictiveness and fear. These are the "men of great stature," those unattractive *giants* (vv. 32–33) that we find living in our own hearts. Through these weeks, we have been "opening our hearts" in order to take a good look at these giants so that we might understand better how to overcome them. We know their intentions and their tactics. By their sheer size and number, they are able sometimes to distract us from the path that is set before us and obscure our vision of the "promised land" that we seek. Their only purpose is to wreak havoc in our souls, to alienate us from our fellow travelers, and to weaken our resolve to follow the One who goes before us. Ultimately, they would like nothing more than to keep us from going the whole distance and finishing our course. But they cannot be allowed to succeed. Not a single one of them is so strong that it cannot be subdued. Their end, however, will be determined to a large extent by how we choose to look at them.

The twelve spies sent into Canaan by Moses brought back a mixed report to the people of Israel. The land before them was spacious and fruitful, "flowing with milk and honey."

They even carried evidence of its abundance for all the people to see—imagine, a single cluster of grapes that took two men to carry! This truly was the land of promise. But ten of the spies also said that this was as close as the people should ever get to it. Their vision fixed upon the frightening inhabitants of the land, and their hearts fainted within them. All they saw was the impossibility of what lay before them, and all they could imagine was the defeat that they feared would inevitably come. But Hoshea (called Joshua) and Caleb saw differently. Even as their eyes saw the same giants as their colleagues, their hearts saw more. "The Lord is with us," they declared; "do not fear them" (14:9). Their resolute counsel was for the people to move forward, to trust in the promises of God and to count upon his strength. The "giants" were no reason to believe that God had changed his mind about what he intended. They only provided another opportunity for the people to depend upon God, and for God to bless his people.

Joshua's advice went unheeded, and so, for forty years, an entire generation of Israelites wandered and perished in the wilderness. A new generation arose, and, with Joshua at their head, they came to enter and inhabit the land of promise. It is to the story of Joshua that we turn as we conclude these twelve weeks of reflections. His name means "God has saved," another form of that name above all names—"Jesus." Joshua is the Old Testament figure of our Savior, who is leading us to our own land of blessing.

Even as we still stand at a distance from the fulfillment of all the good things that God has in store for us (here in the "wilderness of Paran"), Joshua is telling us to keep moving forward. Can you hear his wise and fervent counsel? As you face the close of these twelve weeks, can you look forward and get a glimpse, through your Savior's eyes, of the destiny that lies ahead? He has been to that land already—he walked the entire distance just as we do; he fought with and defeated the same giants that we now face; he laid claim to the promise of his Father; and now he has returned to lead us to our promised home. Can you hear him as he says, "Come, follow me?"

REFLECT | *What are the "giants"—the forces that tempt you to turn back—that you are facing these days? Which one of them are you most discouraged about overcoming? What can you do in order to "keep moving forward"?*

Day 2   Be Strong and of Good Courage

READ | Joshua 1:1–11

Have I not commanded you? Be strong and of good courage; be not frightened, neither be dismayed; for the Lord your God is with you wherever you go." (v. 9)

Forty years after the twelve Israelite spies reported back to Moses at Kadesh, Joshua and a new generation of Israelites stood at the banks of the Jordan River anticipating their entry into the "promised land." A new and unknown venture lay before them—the promise of great blessing together with the certainty of great challenges—and the opening chapter of the Book of Joshua records God's charge to the man whom he had chosen to lead the way. We can hear in these words the voice of God to us as we look forward to taking the next steps of our own pilgrimage.

Three times the Lord repeated to Joshua: "Be strong and of good courage" (vv. 6, 7, 9). Three times in eleven verses. Do you suppose there is a reason? Only God knew what lay before Joshua. God alone had the eyes to see everything that Joshua would face in the coming years—every step, every stumble, every turn, and every straight way. He knew every setback he would suffer, and every victory he would enjoy. He also had no doubt whatsoever about the final outcome.

Joshua, however, was only a man, and therefore too small to see very far ahead. So, the things that he could not possibly know by himself, God told him. He promised him that the land would be won. He reminded Joshua about the law, the words that he had given to his servant Moses, and told him to cling to it and follow it, without diverting from it in any way. This would be the guarantee of his prosperity and success. God told Joshua that there was no reason to be afraid, that he would never have to face alone the difficulties that came against him, and that he, the Lord his God, would be with him wherever he went. These are the reasons for which Joshua could be strong and courageous—because God promised that he would *never* fail or forsake him (v. 5). Can you hear God as he speaks these words to you today, as he calls you to set your sights forward to the next step of the journey?

I will be with you wherever you go—God has faithfully brought you to the place you stand now. You did not set forth on the path, neither did you arrive here under your own strength. Along the way, you have already seen many signs of his love for you and of his ability to help you. Is there any reason to think that he would leave you on your own now?

Be not frightened, neither be dismayed—The Lord your God, the One who has made you his own child, is greater than you can ever imagine. There is nothing that his love cannot accomplish for you. Do not forget that the highest mountains that loom before you look like tiny knolls when seen from heaven.

I will not fail you or forsake you—God has given you every piece of equipment necessary for a successful journey. Even if you cannot find it right now, not one thing will ever be missing when you need it. All you need do is follow the directions that he gives and you are guaranteed to arrive safely at the destination he has in store.

With all this, and so much more, is there any reason that God should hesitate to expect us to *be strong and of good courage?*

REFLECT | *Which of these assuring words means most to you today? What can you do to firmly lay hold of these truths? God must have spoken these words to Joshua because he knew that Joshua might be afraid. What are you most afraid of in the coming weeks?*

Day 3   A New Journey

READ | Joshua 3

When you see the ark of the covenant of the Lord your God being carried by the Levitical priests, then you shall set out from your place and follow it, that you may know the way you shall go, for you have not passed this way before. (vv. 3–4)

When I was a child, my family would sometimes make a traveling vacation that took me to various parts of the country. I look back fondly upon these trips, and remember with a smile one thing that was common to them all—I could not sleep the night before we left. The thought of getting up early in the morning and setting out on the road to a new and different place was too exhilarating to allow sleep. The fun would be in the destination, but it was also in the journey.

Joshua and the people of Israel were camped at the Jordan River. For forty years they had known only the world of the wilderness. Daily life had gone unchanged since the days of their mothers and fathers—setting up camp, taking down camp, gathering manna, praying in the tabernacle—and all the time they were passing by the same scenery and the same landmarks that they had passed by the month before. On this day, however, they awakened to something new and different . . . and totally unknown.

We don't think about it much, but the truth is that each day that greets us is a new step on our path of discipleship. In countless ways, today's scenery will look similar to yesterday's, and we might succumb to the temptation to believe that we've been this way before. But the life of the disciple regularly brings us to the banks of a new Jordan River—new challenges, new successes, new disappointments, new pains, new joys. Some of the experiences that await us this day will be familiar, but others will be dramatically different. There is no way to prepare for them all, only to walk with God through each one of them as we meet them.

Not knowing the things that lie ahead can be both unnerving and exhilarating. What we can know, however, is the way to get there. Under Joshua's leadership the commanders of Israel directed the people essentially to "keep an eye out." The ark of the covenant—representing the presence of God in their midst—would soon pass by and lead them through the river. Watch carefully, they ordered, and do not assume that you know the way. *You have never passed this way before.*

We can be certain that God knows the way that lies before us. There will be no surprises for him today. This is one of the reasons that you and I can face our futures confidently. The way that God prepared the people of Israel for this very new and very big step of their journey was by teaching them to follow him in all the little steps that got them to this point. All the tedious days they had already lived, learning to love and to obey the Lord, were getting them ready for a new adventure that they could not yet imagine. They had already learned to follow the ark. Today it was more important than ever that they do so.

God knows what is coming into our lives. He knows the rivers we will face, and he knows that the only way we will be able to successfully cross each one of them will be by following his lead. The lessons of love and obedience that we learned yesterday and the day before and the day before that were all getting us ready for today. And today will prepare us for tomorrow. Then, when it comes time to cross that last river, we will be ready for the adventure of a lifetime!

REFLECT | *What lessons have you already learned by following Jesus that you are able to put into practice today? What lesson do you think he has been teaching you lately? For you, what does it mean specifically to watch for the ark going before you?*

Day 4   What Do These Stones Mean?

READ | Joshua 4

[Joshua] said to the people of Israel, "When your children ask their fathers in time to come, 'What do these stones mean?' then you shall let your children know, 'Israel passed over this Jordan on dry ground.' " (v. 21)

Do you keep a record of God's blessings and answers to prayer? Some Christians do, and they find the practice enjoyable and reassuring. "Counting your blessings" can be an effective means of shining light into the shadows of discouragement, but it only works if you remember what those blessings are and have been.

We have remarked before that we human beings are prone to "forgetfulness" with regard to the things of God. In the face of present temptations, for example, we often forget the price we paid the last time we gave in. Or in the face of present pain, we forget how God comforted and healed us before. Or in the face of prosperity, we may forget the Source of all our blessings. Consider the numbers of times that the children of Israel were instructed to "remember" what God had done for them. It sounds as if the Lord knew that someday they would forget:

—You shall remember that you were a servant in the land of Egypt. (Deut. 5:15)

—You shall not be afraid of them, but you shall remember what the LORD your God did to Pharaoh and to all Egypt. (Deut. 7:18)

—You shall remember all the way which the LORD your

—God has led you these forty years in the wilderness.
(Deut. 8:2)

—You shall remember the LORD your God. (Deut. 8:18)

—Take heed lest you forget the LORD, who brought you
out of the land of Egypt, out of the house of bondage.
(Deut. 6:12)

Memorials of all kinds are set up in remembrance
of people and events in our history that should never be
forgotten. The memorial itself becomes our connection to
those events and to those people, and, especially when they
have affected us in some personal way, it can elicit from us
a whole array of remembrances, including all the emotions
that come with them. I once visited the small church and
cemetery of my Irish ancestors. Seeing my own name
inscribed on dozens of gravestones, some of which were
hundreds of years old, actually made me feel surrounded
by this long-forgotten family, and, quite unexpectedly, I
was overwhelmed by a deep sense of belonging. Such is the
power of a stone of remembrance.

The stones that the Lord commanded to be set up in the
Jordan were meant to tell the coming generations that they
belonged as well—belonged to a family whose ancestors had
once passed this way; belonged to a people who had once
been miraculously preserved from destruction; belonged
to a God who had once saved them. All those events, and
many, many more, were contained in those twelve stones.
But, in the case of memorials to the work of God, those
events are still going on. The good things that God has done
in the past are but the assurances for what he can do today,
and will most certainly do tomorrow. In a sense, by the

handiwork of God, you and I are now among those "living stones" that our children and our children's children will look to and ask, "What do these stones mean?" And when they ask, may there be someone to answer and say, "These are the reminders to us, that our God is good."

REFLECT | *Make a list of the good things that God has done for you in the last twelve weeks. What does this list tell you about the future?*

Day 5   Do Not Turn Back

READ | Joshua 23

You know in your hearts and souls, all of you, that not one thing has failed of all the good things which the LORD your God promised concerning you; all have come to pass for you, not one of them has failed. (v. 14)

Jumping to the end of the book of Joshua, we find the children of Israel living securely in their new home. Not all the country has been settled, and not every soul is at rest, but Joshua's work is done. He is now the patriarch of the nation, having faithfully wedded this people to their land in the service of God. Joshua has lived up to his name: through his obedience and perseverance, God saved his people for himself.

Joshua now stands before the people "old and well advanced in years," bequeathing to them a blessed future that has been securely built upon God's deeds of the past. Nevertheless, the blessings of the future that Joshua sees are also dependent upon their own deeds, especially their own

obedience and faithfulness to God. Even with their reward
in hand, declares Joshua, they will soon face the temptation
to "turn back" from the ways of God and join with the ways
of those who were once their enemies. Joshua warns that if
they do so, they will be ruined.

The call to perseverance is almost harder to hear in
times of peace than it is in times of adversity. The pain of
suffering usually makes us acutely aware of life's choices and
the sharp differences there are among them. When we are
at our lowest and weakest, we are likely to be super-sensitive
to the temptation to give up and turn back. According to
Matthew's account, it was not until *after* Jesus fasted in the
wilderness for forty days that the tempter came and said to
him, "If you are the Son of God, command these stones to
become loaves of bread" (4:2–3). So long as the people of
Israel were wandering in the wilderness, utterly dependent
upon the water and manna that they found each day and
needing the pillar of fire and cloud to lead them from place
to place, the temptation to turn back to Egypt was blatantly
obvious. But now that they knew prosperity, now that their
stomachs were always full, their lands always fertile, and their
weapons always in the closet, they were especially susceptible
to the more subtle temptations to turn away from God.

Joshua's counsel to Israel is of value to us as well. We
recognize temptation when it comes to us in those structured
times of self-discipline and self-denial. We may still give in to
it, but there is no question about what we are doing. At such
times, it is as if we have placed a fence around us. It leaves us
a very small space in which to move, but we have no trouble
knowing either when we have stepped out of its confining
limits, or when something has stepped in and is crowding

us. But, once that fence is gone, once there are no more obvious "lines to cross," and our moving about becomes freer and easier, then we have a harder time knowing when we have moved in the wrong direction.

The words of Joshua remind us that when this happens (not *if* this happens), we can still turn to the Lord our God and remember the covenant he has made with us. Our futures hold both the structured times and the unstructured. There is no reason that we should not remain faithful to God in both, because God has remained faithful to us.

REFLECT | *What are you most afraid of about "releasing" yourself from various disciplines or restraints? What would it mean for you to be tempted in times of prosperity? What would be your weakest point?*

Day 6   Choose This Day

READ | Joshua 24

Choose this day whom you will serve, whether the gods your fathers served in the region beyond the River, or the gods of the Amorites in whose land you dwell; but as for me and my house, we will serve the Lord. *(v. 15)*

The twenty-fourth chapter of Joshua is like a quick review of the entire history of Israel—a "CliffsNotes" study guide to the old covenant. We, too, have met with some of these figures over the past twelve weeks: Abraham, Jacob and Esau, Moses and the children of Israel. Their lives are among those through whom God established his promise on the earth and advanced his plan of salvation. Joshua rehearses this miraculous and glorious past in order to compel the people to hold fast in the future.

Choose this day whom you will serve. Isn't this the choice that you and I face every day? You must choose, says Joshua, because, whether you consciously intend to or not, you will most surely be serving some god. It will either be the God of all heaven and earth, or it will be one of the gods you met yesterday, or one of the gods you will meet tomorrow. Make no mistake about it, he says. You must choose, because, if you don't serve one of them, then you will be serving the other. So, which one will it be?

Most of us are familiar with times of new resolutions and fervent commitments. We make them at special times like the New Year, or our birthday, or the season of Lent. They are designed to set us upon a specific course of action, defined by a fresh sense of priorities and a renewed vision for what our lives can be like. In other words, they are opportunities to "start over." In a sense, Joshua was presenting the people of Israel with just such an opportunity. But, in his words, we also find that the opportunity is presented every day.

Chose *this* day. We look at Joshua and we admire a man who persevered in his commitment to God under adversity as well as prosperity. But perseverance is measured not by great and noble feats, nor by flash fires of determination. The quality of perseverance is measured by one good choice after another, after another, after another. It is a fruit that takes years to ripen, but those years are still only lived one day at a time.

The life of the people of Israel continued long after Joshua died. We know that the choices that they made through the years were a thorough mixture of good and bad, wise and foolish, faithful and blasphemous. Still, one thing never changed—God was always ready for them to choose him. That would be a daily opportunity, and it still is.

REFLECT | *What will it mean for you to "choose God" each day? Who are some of the other "gods" whom you will be tempted to serve?*

Day 7   A New Creation

READ | Revelation 21–22

And he who sat upon the throne said, "Behold, I make all things new." (21:5)

We began this series of reflections in the opening chapters of the Book of Genesis. It is only fitting that we end it with the closing chapters of the Revelation to John. This is a long way from Joshua, I know, but what took place for the people of Israel by Joshua's hand was only a foreshadowing of what would take place for us by the hand of Jesus. The promised land into which he longs to lead us is unimaginably beautiful, primarily because it is his own home and he will be there. It will be a paradise in which all that was lost in Eden will be found, all that was broken will be mended, all that died will be made alive.

I have heard young mothers say that the excruciating pain of childbirth all but vanished with the first warm feel of their newborn child upon their breast. If the touch of one little child can relieve such hurt, if those gentle fingers can somehow lessen the pain of sin's curse (Genesis 3:16), how much more consolation can we expect from the hands of God's own Child? The vision of heaven that John receives is meant to tell us that the pains we endure have both a purpose and an end.

We have talked a good deal about "goals" over these past twelve weeks. Some of the great teachers of the early church used to talk about goals, too, but they warned against mistaking them for the true end of our lives. The goals that we reach (or fail to reach) in this life are only "sub-goals," as one young person I know put it. John was presenting the true end and purpose of our lives. Like Joshua, he was an old man by the time he saw the "promised land," and well experienced with suffering and pain. Imagine how he must have felt when he received this glimpse of heaven. He tells his readers that this is what makes it all worthwhile. This is the destination for every disciple, and when they reach it, there will be no thought left of the rough road that got them there. In the face of Love himself, how can there be any remembrance of pain?

Saint Augustine said that the suffering we endure on earth is only a sign of our longing for heaven. We are "nostalgic" for home, and our hearts ache so long as we are away. When we open our hearts as we have done through these weeks, we can easily read in them the signs of this nostalgia. This is why we should not allow ourselves to become discouraged when the ache grows so strong. It is only an indication of how deeply we long to be delivered.

For the real birth that is taking place is our own. You and I are the ones being "re-made," being born again into the kingdom of heaven. And the real pain to be borne has been borne already by our Savior who, like Adam, opened his own side in order to bring another life—our life—into his world.

So do not lose heart. Instead, open your heart . . . to the One who makes all things new.

Works Cited

The following books were available in print at the time of this writing. (Works in the public domain are available from numerous sources on the Internet.)

Buttrick, George Arthur, editor. *The Interpreter's Bible* [Editorial board: George Arthur Buttrick, commentary editor, and others]. New York: Abingdon-Cokesbury Press, 1951–57.

Fénelon, François. *The Royal Way of the Cross.* Hal M. Helms, editor. Brewster, MA: Paraclete Press, 1982.

Maclaren, Alexander. *Psalms for Sighs.* Grand Rapids, MI: Wm. B. Eerdmans Pub. Co., 1945.

Meyer, F. B. *Great Verses Through the Bible: A Devotional Commentary on Key Verses.* Grand Rapids, MI: Zondervan, 1972.

Suter, John Wallace, Jr., editor. *The Book of English Collects.* New York: Harper, 1940.

Tickle, Phyllis. *The Divine Hours: Prayers for Autumn and Wintertime.* New York: Image Books, 2006.

Tickle, Phyllis. *The Divine Hours: Prayers for Summertime.* New York, Image Books, 2006.

Must-have Companions
on Your Journey to Wholeness

Your Whole Life JOURNAL
Record your progress with this convenient, inspirational, spiral-bound journal designed for twelve weeks of your 3D journey.

$14.95

Your Whole Life PEDOMETER
Clip this little tool to your waistband or hip pocket and let it become part of your daily discipline.

$12.95

Your Whole Life INSPIRATIONAL CD
Get inspired each morning by a message from Carol Showalter—one for each of the twelve weeks. This engaging, 36-minute CD is also ideal for playing aloud at your weekly meetings.

$16.95

The 3D PRAYER CARD
"Dear Lord, This is a new day . . ." A personal prayer by Carol Showalter, beautifully designed and laminated. Available in packs of 10.

$5.95/pack

THE 3D PLAN

EAT RIGHT • LIVE WELL • LOVE GOD

For more information, go to the 3D website, www.3DYourWholeLife.com, or call 1-800-451-5006.